"Adriaan has spent countless hours in direc
contemporary business leaders. The result i
into their lives, experiences and leadership
of tools and principles for South African mai
influence and take big steps in their lead
reading!"
Grant Ashfield—MD LeadershipWorks

"The first leadership book I have read that is short, to the point, and brilliantly structured. The real-life examples of South African leaders make it all the more relevant."
Gidon Novick—Joint CEO Comair Limited (British Airways & kulula.com)

"Gems of leadership wisdom. Leadership knowledge shared from interactions with top leaders. Practical principles for leadership development of current and aspiring leaders. Inspiring."
Marko Saravanja—Director Regenesys Business School

"Seldom can so many pearls of wisdom from proven South African leaders be condensed into one publication, with all of the key requirements and the attributes of leadership clearly and comprehensively enunciated. This book can help you to positively direct your leadership destiny."
John Barry—Founder of Adcorp and author of *Leading from the front*

"Though a great deal of reliance is placed on leadership experience in the corporate sector, the lessons are applicable across all sectors—political, business and civil-society leaders will benefit from this book. This work is chiefly concerned with identifying principles governing leadership and does this by drawing on the rich experiences of individuals with extensive leadership experience. The principles are distilled from and informed by experiences of practitioners who know their craft well. This book demystifies the concept by demonstrating that leadership can be understood by anyone if the fundamental principles which drive leaders are studied. These principles open the field up to anyone. Leaders and non-leaders will benefit from reading this book."
Khehla Shubane—Former CEO Nelson Mandela Foundation and Non-Executive Director on several boards, including First Rand Bank Ltd

I found the book easy to read—as Adriaan said—on a flight home. I like the summaries at the end of each section and chapter; makes for easy referral when reminding oneself of a point he makes. The fact that the book is made up of Adriaan's views and the experiences of many successful leaders makes it very powerful and real. What impacted me most about the book is that it is actually a book on how to live your life, clearly confirming his opinion that we all need to be leaders in every facet of our lives and if done well will help us to live fuller and more rewarding lives.
Ian McDonald—Sales Director Nestlé South Africa

Published in 2008 by 30° South Publishers (Pty) Ltd.
28 Ninth Street, Newlands, 2092
Johannesburg, South Africa
www.30degreessouth.co.za
info@30degreessouth.co.za

Design and origination by 30° South Publishers (Pty) Ltd.

Printed and bound by Pinetown Printers, Durban

ISBN 978-1-920143-28-2

MOVING TOWARDS YOUR LEADERSHIP DESTINY

Adriaan Groenewald

Contents

ACKNOWLEDGEMENTS

I have held hundreds of formal interviews and discussions on leadership and success in the last few years with top leaders and experts/gurus. These have been both on and off air, with audiences of various sizes. I have written dozens of articles on leadership for recognized newspapers and magazines. I have co-written a book on leadership with my father. I have coached countless people on their journeys to becoming greater leaders.

I remember, several years ago, while I was interviewing a CEO for our first book, *The CEO Leadership Handbook*, a thought crossed my mind—"I am so lucky to be in the presence of 'successful' individuals so often. I wish more people could be in my shoes, to hear what they have to say."

About two years later, I was fortunate enough to start presenting the Leadership Platform on radio. My aspiration then was simply to afford prospective leaders the opportunity to rub shoulders with those who are at the peak of their respective powers. I continue to learn much; only now, others learn with me.

The following list includes some of the individuals who have made a contribution in some form or another in the past few years, and the list continues to grow. In many cases their titles reflect the position held at the time of interview.

Amuah, Dr Kwame—OSR Group chairman

Andersen, Roy—Murray & Roberts, Virgin Active and Sanlam non-executive chairman

Angus, Richard—First National Bank Corporate CFO
Bacher, Dr Ali—former United Cricket Board MD
Barry, John—Adcorp founder
Bauermeister, Karl—FNB HomeLoans New Business CEO
Benvie, Errol—Ebony Consulting International MD
Bernstein, Gavin—Moroka Swallows Football Club director
Berryman, Steve—Square One director
Beukes, Izanne—former ABSA Group Executive Strategy Development
Bickett, Nicky—former Old Mutual GM for HR
Binedell, Prof. Nick—GIBS director
Bluen, Vanessa—The Consultant Powerhouse CEO and Boss of the Year finalist 2005
Blumenthal, Ivor—Services Seta CEO
Botha, David—SA Institution of Civil Engineering executive director and Boss of the Year finalist 2005
Cameron, Gail—Image Excellence CEO
Cavalieri, Paolo—former Hollard Insurance CEO
Clark, Ivan—former Grindrod CEO
Cockerill, Ian—Gold Fields CEO
Coetzer, Garth—Square One chairman
Corlette, Roger—Liberty Properties MD
Covey, Dr Stephen R.—author of *The Seven Habits of Highly Effective People*
Cozens, Ladragh—Cozens Recruitment CEO
Creamer, Tom—Telesure Group director
Da Silva, Peter—former Siemens CEO
Dabengwa, Sifiso—MTN International COO
De Meillon, Eugene—former Hotline Administrative Services MD
Dick, Angela—Transman CEO
Dippenaar, Laurie—co-founder of First Rand Limited
Dockrat, Ismail—Wesgro CEO and Boss of the Year 2005
Donald, Ian—Nestlé Ice Cream MD

Donnelly, Sean—former Genesis Consulting SA MD
Du Plessis, Visser—businessman, TV presenter and actor
Du Toit, Ernest—Avroy Shlain and Swissgarde CEO
Dumas, André—Square Group CEO
Epstein, Ivan—Softline CEO and founder
Fauconnier, Dr Con—Kumba CEO and Boss of the Year 2004
Fenn, Dr Orrie—Pretoria Portland Cement COO
Ferreira, Henry—former Hewlett Packard MD
French, Peter—former Compuware MD
Furphy, Wayne—former Accenture SA MD
Gihwala, Prof. Dines—Hofmeyr Attorneys executive chairman
Golden, Christoffel Jnr—The Church of Jesus Christ of Latter Day Saints South East Africa president
Gore, Adrian—Discovery Health CEO
Groenewald, General Tienie—former military and political leader RSA
Groenewald, Louis—father of author
Groenewald, Rina—mother of author
Grové, Joe—Unitrans CEO
Hall, Colin—Former Wooltru CEO
Hall, Darren—McDonalds MD
Hanratty, Paul—Old Mutual Africa MD
Harris, Mark—IBM SA MD
Harris, Paul—First Rand Limited CEO
Heath, Adv. Willem—Heath Executive Consultants CEO
Hill, Thomas—Integrear CEO
Hilton-Smith, Fran—Women's Football Association president
Hlahla, Monhla—ACSA CEO and Businesswoman of the Year 2005
Hogg, Alec—Moneyweb CEO
Holt, Barry—former Unisys MD
Howell, Philip—former Barclays Bank MD
Johnston, Yvonne—International Marketing Council of SA CEO
Joosub, Shameel—Vodacom MD

Joubert, Mike—Levi Strauss & Co MD
Kaelin, Alfred—former Nestlé CEO
Kast, Ingrid—DAV Professional Placement Services CEO
Knott-Craig, Alan—Vodacom CEO
Kok, Ed—AA MD
Kulula CEO—Gidon Novick
Lamberti, Mark—former CEO Massmart
Lascaris, Reg—TBWA Hunt Lascaris regional president
Lekota, Patrick M.—ANC chairperson and Minister of Defence
Leon, Tony—former Democratic Alliance leader
Letele, Nolo—Multichoice CEO
Liebenberg, Shaun—Denel CEO
Lopez, Alfonzo—author and coach
Lorge, Stan—Computershare CEO
Loubser, Russell—JSE CEO
Lucas-Bull, Wendy—businesswoman
Mabaso, Luke—Safintra executive director
Magau, Dr Namane—former Businesswomen's Association president
Malele, Zeth—former Arivia.com CEO
Manyatshe, Maanda—former MTN MD
Manyi, Jimmy—Black Management Forum president
Mape, Tumi —Union Alliance Holdings CEO
Marcus, Gill—ABSA chair
Maron, Ian—Liberty Corporate Benefits MD
Marupen, Fergus—Kumba Resources HR GM
Mashaba, Herman—businessman and founder of Black Like Me
Mayne, Colin—former Dimension Data I-Commerce MD
McLean, Jim—former Liberty Properties MD
Meiring, Johan—Mayibuye Group CEO
Meyer, Heyneke—Blue Bulls coach
Mohlala, M.K.—former City Power CEO
Mojela, Louisa—Whiphold CEO

Mokaba, Dr Bennie—former Shell South Africa marketing MD
Mokgosi, Thoko—Hewlett Packard CEO
Moloi, Julia—We Are Capable founder & Woman of the Year 2005 in Communication category
Moyo, Peter—former CEO Alexander Forbes
Mzimba, William—Accenture SA MD
Nhleko, Phuthuma—MTN CEO
Nkosi, Duma—Ekurhuleni executive mayor
Nqakula, Charles—Minister of Safety and Security
Oaks, General Robert C.—former military and corporate leader in USA
Otto, René—Channel Life CEO and founder of Outsurance
Pienaar, Francois—former Springbok rugby captain
Pinker, Richard—Gestetner MD
Prahalad, C.K.—author and strategist
Pretorius, Brand—McCarthy Limited CEO
Prins, Leon—Moroka Swallows Football Club CEO
Rall, Prof. Johan—Unisa SBL
Redshaw, David—Fintek CEO
Ritchie, James—Ritchie Enterprises chairman (USA)
Ross, Steve—Edcon CEO
Rowbotham, Rupert—former Reuters MD
Sambane, Henry—Crabtree executive director and Boss of the Year finalist 2005
Scoble, Chris—Nashua MD
Sears, Bill—former Nestlé Ice Cream MD
Serima, Pfungwa—Microsoft MD
Serobe, Gloria—Businesswoman of the Year 2006
Shilowa, Mbhazima—Gauteng Premier
Silverstone, René—Jupiter Drawing Room CEO
Slabbert, Dr van Zyl—Adcorp chairman
Smale, Martin—Liberty Personal Benefits MD
Smith, Colin—South African Communications Union president

Smith, Greg—Genesis Consulting International CEO
Sparks, Roddy—former Old Mutual Africa MD
Stalz, Werner—former ABN Amro Bank MD
Summers, Sean—former Pick 'n Pay CEO
Swanepoel, Bernard—former Harmony Gold CEO
Tiekie, Ouma—99-year-old mother of ten children, and grandmother to many grandchildren and great grandchildren
Twala-Tau, Pilisiwe—City of Johannesburg Region 3 director and Boss of the Year finalist 2005
Vermaak, Frik—former Computershare CEO
Viljoen, Johan—Mponeng Anglogold Ashanti GM and Boss of the Year finalist 2005
Volkwyn, Terry—Primedia Broadcasting CEO and Boss of the Year 2006
Wakeford, Kevin—former SACOB CEO and now Eastern Cape Development Corporation CEO
Walker, Howard—Alexander Forbes MD
Watt, Peter—Comparex CEO
Webber, Bill—former Cisco MD SA
Wepener, Annelize—*CEO Magazine* founder and CEO
White, Dayle—Flight Centre MD
Wilford, Colin—clinical psychologist and executive coach
Woods, Ted—former Deutsche Bank CEO
Woolfson, Alan—former Charter Life MD
Zille, Helen—Democratic Alliance leader

Many other informal meetings and interviews have been held over the years. I am grateful for the contributions of the above, as well as those of many other people.

It needs to be mentioned that the listed leaders and others merely contributed to my thinking and understanding of what being a successful leader is all about. I therefore do not necessarily hold up each person as having been constant examples of the principles discussed in this book.

Another important acknowledgement is that although mostly prominent individuals in important positions are listed above, I certainly do not imply that I have only learned about leadership from them. Doing so would suggest that one can only learn from individuals in recognized positions, which is not the case.

I further believe that a lot of what we learn regarding successful leadership stems from the home. Great fathers and mothers are usually great people and leaders. I have incredible parents from whom I have learned a great deal. In fact, my father and I wrote *The CEO Leadership Handbook* together. A lot of my thinking stems from our association, and the more I connect with great leaders the more I am convinced of those principles contained in our first book.

Finally, at no point do I claim to live by all or even most of the principles in *Moving Towards Your Leadership Destiny*, but I do try to live by such standards. Sometimes I succeed and at other times I fail.

Adriaan Groenewald
Centurion, Gauteng
March 2008

INTRODUCTION

Purpose of the book

Behind me in my home office hangs a framed photograph—a gift from my business partner, Sean Donnelly, and his wife Dianne. It is a photograph of me standing next to Dr Stephen R. Covey, the renowned author of *The Seven Habits of Highly Effective People* and many other books. Recently, I had the privilege of interviewing him in his hotel room in Sandton. The room was rather modest compared to my expectations of where this icon in his field would be staying. In fact, we battled to find the space to arrange three cameras for Summit TV!

I remember meeting him in the passage on his way to his room. He had just spent a full day with 1,000 business executives. He smiled at me and seemed to have energy left in him. I joked by commenting that he could spend another few hours with a thousand more executives. The man is in his seventies, yet walked into his room and sat down, almost in pre-programmed fashion, ready for yet another interview. In fact, I asked him off air if he sometimes felt like a robot, moving from one event or interview to the next. He answered with childlike honesty that he did sometimes feel like a robot.

I have often found over the years that the moments before and after formal interviews have been the most special, as was the case with Dr Covey. I looked into this man's eyes, which were clear blue, and I could sense that he was a good man with good motives and desires. Sitting in the same room with him, I was able to sense things the audience would not be able to while watching the interview on television or listening on radio. This has been my blessing over the years—to be taught about successful leadership on and off air and then to go out there and apply some of it myself and to teach others. Some leaders taught me more about how to be successful as individuals and leaders during the pre-show meetings—through the questions they would ask, or the questions they would not ask; through their actions and behaviour towards me and those around them; through simply being themselves off camera and microphone.

I met Angela Dick, founder and CEO of Transman and Businesswoman of the Year in 2006 at her office, which happens to be next to her home. She ended up taking me on a tour of her character-filled home, which taught me more about her than the 40-minute interview and pre-meeting.

Every now and then, I feel like pinching myself when I have the time to sit down and clearly reflect on who I have met, interviewed and associated with over the years. The word 'pinch' reminds me of the charismatic Matthews Phosa who said, as only he can and while exploring why he is able to relate to all people, that, "We are all human beings. If you pinch me I feel pain. If you pinch President Thabo Mbeki he will feel the same pain. There is no presidential pain. It is all human pain …"

Such experiences with Dr Covey, Angela Dick, Matthews Phosa, and too many others to share, made me want as many people as possible to benefit from what I have learned regarding leadership from successful and sometimes not so successful leaders. My greatest desire was to produce a book that was not too thick and that could describe these magnificent principles in the shortest, most concise manner; a book that leaders could actually finish reading and not give up on because it was simply too thick. I asked Dr Covey if his books were not too long and he agreed. He said that if he had to write *The Eighth Habit* again it would be much thinner.

After this adventurous and truly exciting road that I have travelled and continue to travel, I feel I can confidently make certain statements, claims and even recommendations regarding leadership. Some of what I have to say may not sit comfortably with those who view themselves as experts on the subject matter. In general, however, I have full confidence that what I will share with you will assist you in moving closer towards your leadership destiny of becoming a greater leader.

To start off with

To start off with, what astounds me is that society at large, and even the so-called experts, seem to be at odds about how one should develop leaders, or even really what leadership is all about!

During one of my latest on-air discussions about this topic, Pete Laburn, a seasoned business executive, and Colin Hall, the former CEO of Wooltru, were in agreement that society is not united as far as leadership development is concerned. As Laburn said: "The notion of leadership is hopelessly misunderstood …"

Hall felt that society is not even united around the definition of leadership.

Ironically, society seems to be quite clear on how to train professionals such as attorneys, engineers, doctors, teachers and nurses. However, when it comes to training or developing leaders, there seem to be as many ways to do this as there are ways to make money! Why? What is going on? Why should leadership be so mythical? Why can we not unite in our efforts to improve and ensure the existence of this all-important societal skill in the future?

Amidst all of this, it is rather interesting to also consider the following questions—why does everyone have an opinion about leadership; about how to lead; about good and bad leadership? Is it because everyone has been led somewhere in their lives? Is it because every single person is being led at any given moment in time? Is it because every person is in fact a leader? Is it all of the above?

I believe it is all of the above, but of more significance is the largely undiscovered truth that almost every person is in fact a leader! Let me explain. In general, leaders are in the business of movement—be it of themselves, others, attitudes, ideas, organizations or countries. I have shared this principle with hundreds if not thousands of leaders and they always agree—a primary function of a leader is to generate movement, more commonly referred to as change, growth or development.

If you are in agreement that creating movement is a primary function of a leader, then the following is also true. If you are an average day-to-day attorney, you are leading cases, organizations and people towards certain legal solutions, which means you create movement. If you are an average day-to-day parent, you are leading your children towards a certain belief system or value system, and teaching them skills to help them cope in life, which means you create movement. If you are a manager in an organization, you are trying to lead your staff to perform better and you are striving to improve the output of whatever you do, which means you create movement. In all of the above cases you are a leader! Somewhere in your life you act as a leader, mostly on a day-to-day basis.

One often hears the definition, and it was emphasized by Laburn and Hall, that you are is not a leader unless someone follows you. Hall said, "The absolute fundamental of leadership is followership."

Well, if someone follows your advice as a doctor, teacher or parent, are you a leader, even though they don't formally 'report' to you? Of course you are! In other words, if you cause movement with someone following you, your advice, or your opinion, then you are a leader!

Can you see why almost every person has an opinion about leadership, no matter how basic it may be? In other words, you not only have an opinion about leadership because you see others being leaders. You have an opinion because you are already a leader. You may just be unconscious of it, mostly because society is confused or, at best, not united about what a leader is.

Hall said, "Every one of us is constantly experiencing our own leadership capability or others on us."

The real debate

Please understand that the debate is no longer who is a leader, because we all are! The debate is no longer whether leaders are born or made, because we are all born! The debate is no longer what a leader does, because we are all in the business of movement, as you will discover in Chapter Three. The real debate is how to get people to accept and believe that they are already leaders and then how to become great leaders—how to build on their current leadership skills or capabilities to generate more effective movement, thus becoming a more effective leader.

Bottom line, whatever you perceive your career or role to be, you are that and a leader—salesperson and a leader, clerk and a leader, teacher and a leader, attorney and a leader, mother and a leader, and so on. The sooner you realize and believe this truth, the sooner you can consciously focus on your journey towards great leadership. This, in many cases, involves either becoming responsible for other people through giving birth, by being promoted or simply by standing out among your peers as a doctor or attorney.

For Hall, a great leader "has a capacity to create high energy followership—he understands what enables people to follow him."

Laburn commented, "A leader, by who he or she is, by what they may or may not know, is able to influence other people, without even trying. Other people choose to seek and follow that influence by virtue of who that person is and the knowledge they might have."

A practical example would be where Doctor One tells me what to do in a cold and clinical way and I have to listen purely because of his technical knowledge—his mannerisms and way of communicating are condescending and irritating. Doctor Two persuades me in a caring, patient and simple way to want to follow his advice and change or move my situation because it will enhance my quality of life and assist me in being a better husband, father and author.

Doctor One is a leader because he gets me to move and Doctor Two is a great leader because he combined technical expertise or knowledge with people skills and then motivated me (increased my energy) by linking it with my values and aspirations to be a better husband, father and author.

The same example applies in the corporate environment or as a parent—you either get staff or children to move because you determine their benefits, income and future or you persuade them to move because they want to.

In my view, great leaders mostly apply the same people and life skills that most people (leaders) apply daily, but they simply do it more effectively. As an example, everyone communicates, but great leaders communicate more effectively. All or most people want to be successful, but great leaders want it with more passion. Everyone listens, but great leaders listen more effectively.

Further to this, Hall and Laburn concurred that one cannot become a great leader without going through a self discovery process of finding out who you are and what is really important to you—self mastery; personal effectiveness; and so on. Hall explained that that leads one to "interpersonal mastery that is EQ [Emotional Intelligence—people and life skills] … and from there you get into team mastery [evolved people skills]."

During a recent interview with Jimmy Manyi, president of the Black Management Forum, we discussed the shortage or not of leadership talent in South Africa. Of course, Manyi is very well known in some circles for his view that the main reason for the slow pace of transformation in corporate South Africa is the racist attitude of mostly white managers. He is yet another leader I wish more people could engage with on a personal level. Following my interview with him, we had a much deeper discussion around his and my views and I found him very accommodating and willing to accept another's point of view. After some debate, we agreed that another possible obstacle, other than racism, is the attitude that you cannot be a leader or manager in an area or industry where you have no formal qualification or knowledge.

In other words, a large law firm will believe that their CEO must be someone from the legal fraternity; no one else can do it! If a black non-attorney therefore applies for the CEO post and is blocked or not accepted, it is easy to shout 'racism'! But, my view is that that same firm would also block a white non-attorney applicant! Racism is, therefore, not the motivator in this instance but rather an unflinching belief that you must be an experienced attorney to run the firm.

This is, however, not entirely true. A seasoned leader without a legal background could do it. Yes, it would be easier to do it with a legal background, but having a legal background does not automatically ensure great leadership. In fact, the legal background could be the largest obstacle to the person being a great leader for the attorney firm!

Many years ago, when Laurie Dippenaar, co-founder of First Rand Group, and his partners took over Momentum, a deal they describe as their first really big step, he went in there to take the lead. Remember that this was not the Dippenaar we know today. This was his first real leadership challenge and he knew nothing about the insurance industry. What did he do? He asked lots of simple questions, because he had to! Today, some believe that that period in which he asked so many questions about the business to try and understand the main drivers was extremely valuable to them! It actually made the leaders think about their business in a different way. It created a culture of asking questions and challenging the process. It created a culture of openness. It created a culture of liberation. It created a culture in which future leaders could blossom.

Despite this example, I made it clear to Manyi during the interview that I believe it takes an extraordinary person to act the way Dippenaar did—to be an outstanding leader in an environment where you have no or little technical expertise. Such a person would have to have had many other experiences along his life path that matured him to a point where he feels confident enough to ask 'stupid' questions; where he feels comfortable about himself as a person, even in an environment where he is not the expert.

In other words, the real leadership debate should also revolve around how to fast-track individuals through a process where they can act like Dippenaar—this can be done! While technical skills will always play an important role in leadership, I believe a lack of understanding in society in general about how to fast-track leadership skills results in too much emphasis being placed on the importance of technical skills.

As you read, ponder and apply the principles in *Moving Towards Your Leadership Destiny*, you will certainly fast-track your journey towards becoming a greater leader!

Definition of great leadership

After many years of debate and pondering the definition of great leadership, I believe it is as follows—the art of moving people and situations profitably. Think about this definition for a moment! To move people, for example, would imply a leader must first learn how to move their attitudes. On the surface, 'moving attitudes' means transforming a negative perception or outlook about a situation to a positive perception or outlook. Thereafter, the leader can move the people and the situation more successfully. Some leaders seem to be able to move situations rather adequately, but they battle to move the people within those situations as effectively. In such instances, the relevant people simply move because their leader has positional power over them. If it weren't for the formal position of their leader, they would not have moved. Great leadership is about creating 'profitable' movement where all stakeholders want to move and where all parties perceive the future and defined outcome as successful. David Noko, the CEO of De Beers Consolidated Mines, was asked what his responsibility is as a leader and part of his answer was "... delivering value to the shareholders and making employees want to do it."

The ANC elections in December 2007 are a magnificent example of this 'attitude management' principle. President Thabo Mbeki was not very successful in moving the attitude or perceptions of the electorate towards him from negative to positive. In fact, he seemed surprised by the fact that he had lost his grip. The result was losing the elections. Mbeki's greatest weakness as a leader may very well be the inability to manage attitudes of people rather than situations. I will go into this in greater detail in later chapters.

I have discovered that most great leaders apply certain universal laws subconsciously. In other words, they don't know that they are applying them. This has some clear implications. For example, how do you consciously transfer or improve something that you do subconsciously?

Once again, these laws that you will read about are as universal as the Law of Gravity and are therefore applied by most 'ordinary' individuals, who are, as discussed earlier, also leaders, but great leaders simply apply them more effectively.

The more I understand leadership, the more I realize that one can learn from a child how to be a great leader, which was the case with me. I believe that children often portray the universal laws and principles defined in this book far more effectively than so-called grown-ups. Unfortunately, society does not necessarily recognize it in them and therefore overlooks their further development. As a result of this, some children probably un-learn and later in their lives have to re-learn the principles.

A couple of years ago, on a Sunday afternoon and following a lovely, filling lunch, my then five-year-old son Roche suggested that I and my brother, Christo, join him for tea. Neither of us felt like doing this as our stomachs were full and our eyelids were heavy. But, he still managed to move us to sit down with him at his miniature table and chairs for after-lunch tea. This was a form of leadership typical of children. If not consciously recognized, what will happen to it?

I echo the sentiments of Adrian Gore, CEO of Discovery, who is adamant that any person can accomplish great things and become successful—it is a choice. As CEO, he attends induction sessions with new employees where he asks the question: "Is there greatness within you?" and every single person answers 'yes'. He has never met someone who doesn't believe there is something special inside them! He always asks a follow-up question to the effect of: "Have you used this greatness?" When he asks attendees this question, they always answer 'no'. He then asks them: "What are you waiting for?"

Well, I ask you the same questions, slightly adapted. Is there greatness within you? Have you started moving towards this greatness, which I believe to be synonymous with great leadership?

Take it or leave it ('TiLi')

You saw or heard about the book *Moving Towards Your Leadership Destiny* and decided to 'take it'. It was your choice! I think you made the right choice, of course. As you read through the book, you will be faced with the choice of applying or not applying the principles—you can Take it or Leave it—'TiLi'. I will share with you my thoughts and feelings about certain prominent individuals in our country and beyond—TiLi. This is what life is all about. You can take to heart what someone tells you, or you can leave it. You can take opportunities or you can leave them. You can do things the way you have always done them and expect different results, or you can start doing things differently and so change the results. It is up to you.

Enjoy the journey, and remember—TiLi!

"Life is essentially about confidence"

CHAPTER ONE

CONFIDENCE

What is confidence?

Before I address the universal laws that great leaders apply mostly subconsciously, I want to cover the principle of confidence. I love writing in my journal and a short while ago I made the following comment about confidence.

"I realized today, more than before, that most human beings, if not all, are not nearly as confident as they project ..."

Think for a moment whether you agree with this statement. All of us realize instinctively how important it is to come across as confident on our journey through life. So, what do we often do? We act confident, or we act out through body language, how we dress or verbally what we perceive confidence to be.

I believe the challenge we face is that, in general, there exist huge misunderstandings about what confidence is! When is someone confident? Are those individuals who outwardly come across as confident really confident? How do you actually develop your confidence? Does the concept of self-confidence in fact exist? I believe most people are confident to some degree, in some context, but great leaders seem more confident more often!

The Green Mile is a film that played on the circuit some time back. I believe this film demonstrates effectively the essence of what confidence is all about. Tom Hanks is the lead actor and plays the role of a supervisor of death row in a 1930s prison.

Michael Clark Duncan plays the role of a huge black man on death row who is falsely convicted of killing two young girls, during a time when race was more of an issue in the USA. He comes across as uneducated, shy, and lacking in confidence. It turns out that he has a certain healing power.

The wife of a senior Correctional Services manager outside the prison contracts brain cancer. Tom Hanks' character and his team decide to secretly take the prisoner to the home of the manager, who is not fully aware of the prisoner's ability, to try and heal his wife.

A scene unfolds where this so-called shy, uneducated, unsure man walks towards the front door of the house while the manager points a shotgun at him. The prisoner confidently moves forward until he is very close to the manager. He slowly and confidently takes the gun from him and says in a deep voice, "I just want to help." He walks past the manager into the home, while the wife screams and groans in pain in the background. The manager runs up from behind shouting at the prisoner to leave his house. The prisoner confidently and gently tells him, "You be quiet now," and he walks up the stairs. Everyone follows him. He heals the wife, and the story continues.

This is an excellent example of the principle that confidence is essentially about trust in processes/abilities/skills/knowledge. When this large 1930s black man moved towards those healing processes or abilities in which he had absolute trust, he suddenly came across as being outwardly confident. Those around him couldn't do anything but follow him. He became the leader. Was he self-confident? No! Did he have trust in a healing process or ability that worked in the past? Yes! The result? He came across as confident when trusting his abilities and the role theyplayed in the healing process.

A person that is well qualified in the field of marketing, and has a great deal of experience in the same field, will come across as very confident when he finds himself in the middle of a discussion on the same topic. Is the individual self-confident? No, not necessarily. He simply has trust in his marketing skills, knowledge and the processes that he has tried in the past and that have worked, like the prisoner on death row trusted his ability to heal. How confident would this same marketer come across if the topic of discussion changed to that of finance? Probably not as confident. The chartered accountant will suddenly come across as more confident, because he or she trusts the financial skills, knowledge and the processes that he or she has successfully applied in the past.

There are so many individuals who are recognized by society as 'confident' and 'successful' because of their position or title and certain material possessions. Often, these people are in fact confident in the context of a certain technical field of expertise—they have mastered principles, processes and knowledge in, for example, law, medicine, engineering or business. The result is that they do become successful, but are they confident beyond their technical expertise? Are they self-confident in general? When one measures them outside of their field of expertise, they are not always confident, or even happy. Examples of this are too many to mention. But I think of a very successful attorney whose home environment is in shambles; I think of a financial director who is in that position because of his expertise, but when it comes to people issues he fails dismally; I think of well-known business individuals who are already on their third or fourth marriages; I think of highly profitable or successful individuals who are alcoholics.

I have come to the conclusion, from personal experience and from my many interviews and associations with prominent individuals, that you can only become a greater leader if you develop confidence (acquire trust in knowledge, skills, principles and processes) in two other areas over and above technical—people interaction and life.

You must acquire trust in knowledge, skills, principles and processes that govern interaction with people and that govern life—TiLi.

Great leaders who come across as confident are not necessarily confident themselves, or self-confident. They are often very aware of their weaknesses and shortcomings. But, they have confidence to engage people and to engage life, over and above technical confidence. Others look at them and see outward confidence, success and happiness, not realizing that what they see is the product of someone who has acquired, or is striving to acquire, trust in principles and processes that drive these three areas.

For example, a very important process you have to master in order to increase your confidence in engaging life is 'getting to know yourself'. You have to follow certain principles and processes to become comfortable with yourself. During an interview with Nolo Letele, CEO of Multichoice, I discussed this principle with him and my panel, Sean Donnelly and Grant Ashfield. Letele felt that, "One should not neglect the spiritual component, not necessarily in the sense of Bible punching or attending church specifically, but being 'centered' and comfortable inside about one's spiritual values."

Donnelly commented that sometimes you need to fix something in your life that is 'bugging' you, before you will feel comfortable inside—clear the conscience.

Ashfield felt strongly about knowing yourself in order to feel comfortable with yourself. He said, "The first thing is knowing yourself—we can't escape ourselves … look in the mirror and ask, 'Who am I; what is my life all about; what are the basic principles that guide my life?' We can't escape that … We can have external success, but do we have internal significance?"

Donnelly added, "The challenge people have in feeling comfortable with themselves is they compare themselves with other people … Don't do that as there will always be someone better … Know yourself; be yourself … do your best!"

Practically, I believe you can get to know yourself by writing in a journal regularly—your thoughts, feelings, desires, and observations. Ashfield mentioned that a practical way to get to know yourself is to "… surround yourself with people you trust and can give you honest feedback."

There are many processes you can follow to get to know yourself and feel comfortable with your strengths and weaknesses. Make the effort so that you can move closer towards becoming a greater leader—TiLi.

Brand Pretorius, the CEO of McCarthy Limited, seems to be an individual who is confident in all three areas of technical, people and life. On 19 April 2007, I interviewed him and made the following entry in my journal.

"When I did my pre-interview research on Brand, I already realized that I was about to meet a special man. Meeting Brand was all and more than I expected. Just by being what he is, he influences others. He lifted me personally by listening with interest after asking questions about me, my dad and our business. People really are number one in his life! When I look at the three areas in which great leaders are confident, he is very strong in all those areas—technical, people and life. He demonstrates two attributes in each area—competence and passion. In other words, he is competent in the motor industry and he loves it; he is brilliantly competent with people and he loves them; and he is competent at life and he loves it! I can go on and on about this man, but, just by being what he is, he influenced and inspired me!"

Enjoying life

Great leaders generate feelings of passion and enjoyment in themselves and others, mostly as a result of their healthy confidence. You can sense this in their presence. What a significant difference it makes when someone is enthusiastic and confident! What a difference it makes to them personally as well as to the people around them.

I had the privilege of being a judge on the 'Boss of the Year' panel. I also interviewed for the first time ever every one of the finalists on the Leadership Platform prior to them appearing before the panel of judges. Their passion and enjoyment for the job and life stood out so clearly. What impressed me even more was the passion and enjoyment that radiated from each one of the nominators while the panel interviewed them. It was clear that these finalists managed to transfer their enjoyment for the job and life over to their staff. Daniel Goleman, author of *Emotional Intelligence* and *The New Leaders*, found in his research that successful leaders generate a resonance of good feelings in those they lead; and that it is this positivity that frees the best in people.

If you want to move towards your destiny of becoming a great leader, you have to acquire an attitude of approval, admiration and acceptance of universal laws, principles and processes that empower you, others around you and situations to move profitably (successfully). The more you focus on universal (always applicable) laws, principles, processes and standards that lead to confidence and success in all areas, the more you will boost your capacity to feel in control and be positive about your challenges—no matter what the situation. You will also be less sensitive about personal feelings and image because you will be so busy measuring your actions against these, rather than against what others think. A great leader does not have emotional hang-ups because his or her focus is on universal laws, principles, processes and standards, rather than emotional self-involvement. This approach tends to allow him or her to be more teachable, to develop a fine sense of humour and to be more relaxed. It provides him or her with emotional space to respect and listen to others.

What other signs may follow a leader who feels secure inside; who radiates a quiet internal confidence as opposed to an external facade? He or she will not motivate by fear but communicate by persuading or 'selling' the message where at all possible.

This seems to be Letele's style. He explains that when a leader takes on such an approach "... both parties come away with conviction about a shared and common goal. For me, I find that works much better because the relationship is good."

Great leaders thoroughly enjoy being exposed to ideas that improve their own performance. They want to know why and how other leaders do well, not to compete, but to discover or broaden their understanding of universal laws, principles, processes and standards, in order to more accurately measure their own performance against these. I seldom find great leaders unapproachable. In fact, I find them surprisingly teachable and even humble.

Lessons learned

Confidence is essentially about trust in your processes, abilities, skills and knowledge.

To be a great leader you must develop confidence in three areas:

1) Technical

2) People interaction

3) Life

Great leaders generate feelings of passion and enjoyment in themselves and others.

The essence of great leadership is an attitude of approval, admiration and acceptance of universal laws, principles, processes and standards that empower you and others around you to move profitably with confidence.

You see, life is essentially about confidence and you need to possess it in order to move towards your leadership destiny. But, not any kind of confidence will do. It requires a specific kind of confidence. In the chapters that follow, I will demonstrate that real confidence is fundamentally about trust in universal people interaction and life processes or laws that lead to successful movement of people and situations. Where trust in such laws, principles and processes dwindle, or in instances where these are not consciously known, situations may be perceived as complicated and confusing. The more complicated and confusing situations appear to a person, the more mistakes are made and the more stress is generated in his or her life—TiLi.

CHAPTER TWO

'EDO' FACTOR

"The difference between a great and a mediocre leader is often determined by the degree of simplicity with which he or she views life"

'Edo' factor

When I speak to an audience, I often ask the following two questions, and I suggest you answer them yourself before you read further.

1) Is life simple or complex?

2) Is life easy or difficult?

What do you think? Right from the outset I suggest your answers should be as follows:

1) Life is simple.

2) Life is difficult.

You see, life consists of innumerable situations every single day; in fact, too many to count. Your task is to move these situations forward profitably or successfully; that is, if you want to reach your destiny of becoming a greater leader! If you agree with this statement, you may think it proves that life is actually very complex. But, let me share with you the first universal law that great leaders apply subconsciously, and allow me to emphasize that by universal I mean a concept that is always applicable anywhere and everywhere, like the Law of Gravity. The law is as follows: All situations in life consist of only two universal actions—evaluate and 'do'.

Is it possible that every one of the myriad situations you face daily can consist of only two over-arching actions? Yes it is! In any given situation all human beings (leaders) either evaluate or 'do', or both. Great leaders evaluate and 'do' more effectively!

My father and I call this principle the 'Edo' factor. You are never ever busy with more than these two actions! When you stop at a stop street, you evaluate to the left, right, front and back and then you 'do'—you drive off. As you read this book you are predominantly in evaluation mode, although you are busy doing something. Think of any situation and try to establish whether or not you are ever not evaluating or doing, or both. Even when you are sitting quietly, you are doing, and you are probably thinking about something, which means you are evaluating. You and I use many different words or synonyms to describe 'evaluate'—assess, think through, consider, ponder, weigh up or appraise. We also use many words to describe 'do'—act, move, apply, react, perform, accomplish, carry out, achieve or execute. But, the fact remains that situations and, therefore, life are actually very simple—they are about continuously evaluating and doing.

If you really want to take the time, you can turn to the person nearest to you and discuss this 'Edo' factor with him or her. In fact, I dare you to try and disprove the law that every single situation in life consists of only two universal actions—evaluate and 'do'. Take on the challenge or leave it—TiLi!

Adrian Gore, CEO of Discovery Health, mentioned to me that he evaluates up to the very last possible moment, until it is almost too late to 'do'. Most profitable and happy leaders have an instinctive respect for 'Edo'. They are not too lazy to evaluate or to 'do'! The 'problem' nowadays is that we want immediate gratification. We actually become lazy evaluators.

Mark Lamberti, founder of Massmart, and now the non-executive chairman, says that there are only three things that really distinguish successful people from non-successful people, no matter what field they are in:

1) Successful people listen to what the world is telling them, and the

world is talking to them all of their waking hours—by way of newspapers, television and radio, and feedback from friends.

2) Successful people interpret what the world is telling them in so far as how significant it is themselves.

3) Successful people do something about it.

He explained that, in his experience, successful people do all three and, as they do, their ability to apply sound judgment improves. His belief in this model coincides with the 'Edo' factor. One could argue that both listening to what the world is telling you and interpreting it are sub-categories of the universal function to evaluate. How do you interpret without evaluating?

You see a great leader manages to patiently evaluate until he or she sees the simplicity in all things, be it a specific situation, an organizational structure, a system, a method of communication, or life in general. Albert Einstein said that any fool can make a simple thing complicated. It takes a genius to make a complicated thing simple. Most of the great leaders I meet are where they are because they have in some way come to see life as relatively simple.

I love the following parable because it illustrates the value of simplicity. A successful farmer sends his son to study at an overseas university. The field of study is nuclear physics. Two years later, the son comes home for the summer holidays and finds himself next to his father on the tractor. His father tries to make conversation with his son by asking him a question, "So, son, tell me what you have learned during the past two years."

The son replied, "Dad, I can't explain quickly here on the tractor what I have learned during the past two years. The field of study that I am pursuing is a complex and difficult one. You won't understand if I tried to explain it to you."

The father keeps quiet for a while and then makes the following wise statement, "So what you are actually telling me, son, is that you don't understand it yet."

The principle is that, once you have simplified a situation or a subject, through effective evaluation, you can explain it. The challenge that all of us face, though, is that the environment around us seems to become more complex—like the son of the farmer with his studies. We are faced with more and more information, technological developments and social complexities. Yet, we are supposed to make decisions so that situations can move forward. But we cannot make decisions in complexity. We have to evaluate through complexity, arrive at the simplicity of the situation—understand the situation or subject matter—make a decision, and then confidently 'do'.

I repeat the principle that the difference between a great and a mediocre leader is often determined by the degree of simplicity with which he or she views life.

'Edo' obstacles

There are many obstacles or even traps we fall into that prevent confident and effective 'Edo' from occurring, or that make this simple life principle difficult. Some of these became more obvious to me after spending quality time with the author and coach, Alfonzo Lopez, who I mention in more detail inthe last chapter. I will discuss just a few and I am sure you can come up with more.

Ignorance

What makes it difficult to confidently and effectively 'Edo' is the fact that sometimes we don't know how to evaluate accurately or successfully. Many of us don't have conscious 'Edo' models or processes that we trust implicitly, so we take unnecessary time and procrastinate or we simply make critical mistakes. We often under evaluate a situation and, when we do, some unexpected curve balls hit us from the side. Or, we over evaluate situations and miss out on opportunities or effective 'doing'.

By ignorance, I also mean 'lack of knowledge' about the situation or various components of the situation. Today, as I write this chapter, exactly a year ago a terrible tsunami caught several countries by surprise. As I watched a documentary on what happened, it reminded me what devastating effects technical ignorance can have. Many of the people did not know that one wave would be followed by another, and yet another. This resulted in ignorance; a lack of knowledge that led to poorer evaluation, ultimately costing them dearly. Yes, granted in some cases this knowledge would not have helped, but in several others it would have given someone just enough of an edge to 'do' the right thing. Some people even noticed that the tides had pulled back very suddenly and that they had never seen this happen before, but they did not know this was a clear sign of a possible tsunami. What would I do should I ever be in such a situation? I will have just a little bit more technical information to confidently 'Edo' more effectively.

Lack of technical knowledge of a specific product or industry could prevent you from knowing what direction to take as a leader of an organization or department. You would have to call on the expertise of others or suffer the consequences of moving in the wrong direction.

Lack of knowledge may also have to do with not understanding people or life laws and principles. When you lack knowledge on the technical side, it is actually easy, relative to lacking knowledge about people dynamics and life. Technical knowledge you can read up on or call on someone who is an expert in the field. Most of the studying that we do at universities and other institutions equips us with some sort of technical knowledge. But, when it comes to people and life, it is more difficult. Most of us do not take the time to understand the universal elements that drive people interaction or govern life, but you need not acquire a psychology degree for this. The rest of this book will go a long way in helping you in this department.

Pressure to act quickly

Another element that makes it more difficult to confidently and effectively 'Edo' is constant pressure to act quickly. Everyone expects answers now!

We live in a world where, when the president and leader of our country decides to take some time to evaluate what he should do about his deputy president's future because of possible involvement in a corrupt relationship, we get impatient, or we jump to conclusions. We want him to tell us right now what he is going to do about the situation! The truth is that the more diverse the aspirations of important stakeholders are—ANC, SACP, COSATU, opposition parties and capitalists—the more difficult it is to evaluate, and the more time is required. Today, with the power of hindsight, one wonders whether the president applied the 'Edo' factor effectively in this instance.

How often do you have someone—wife, child or staff member—rush up to you and present you with a difficult situation or give details of a problem, followed by a question: "What should I do?", expecting an answer there and then? But, how often do you then ask for more information in order to evaluate more effectively? You may reply with—"Hold on, hold on, let's think this through for a moment" or "Have you considered chatting to so and so?" Instinctively, you feel that it is not yet time to move into 'do' mode.

There are so many examples of this in our family lives. While writing this specific chapter, we are on holiday in Hermanus. The morning after our arrival, my wife presented me with a situation. Her father, a retired engineer who has been called back into the profession because of his expertise, was leaving for work in about five minutes. My wife, Melissa, thought it was a good idea for her to spend time with her dad—you know, drive around with him, chat, be away for the day, etc. It was to be his last day of work in Cape Town. She explained her idea to me and asked what I thought—should she go? How often are you confronted with such a situation? You are placed under pressure to decide there and then what to do, but you feel uncomfortable making a decision. The reason you feel uncomfortable is because instinctively you need to evaluate a little bit more, which we started doing. I told my wife that we didn't have enough time to evaluate effectively. I felt uncomfortable making a decision for the sake of it. In fact, we'd just started evaluating when her father left the house and got into his car. That effectively settled the matter. It so happens that her father experienced some complications and could not come home. He had to sleep over for the night, which means my wife would also have had to sleep over. We realized that her idea would not have been ideal.

Urgency

We also live in a world where 'urgency' has become a syndrome—almost an illness. We are driven by it! If you are not busy with urgent issues, you are at risk of being seen as 'not successful' in life. We often run around doing many urgent things, but seldom attend to important and proactive issues. Our minds are cluttered with too many things to do. This urgency mode can impact negatively on 'Edo'.

Anger

Another obstacle to effective and confident 'Edo' is anger. When you evaluate while angry, the action that follows will almost always result in regret. If you have seen the movie *Alexander the Great*, you will remember that he killed one of his trusted advisors at a social gathering during a rage of anger, and of course drunkenness. The regret afterwards was indescribable! You may not end up killing someone, but your action will too often be followed by feelings of regret. An emotion such as anger blocks effective evaluation of a situation because it robs you of a state of peace and clarity of mind, which are crucial for effective 'Edo'. Al Lopez, author of *Multiply Your Total Capacity in Twenty Minutes*, says: "The more clear and peaceful your mind becomes, the more of the whole picture you are able to see, and the better decisions you can make ... A clear and peaceful mind unleashes great power." This is so true. I recently started coaching the senior team of an international engineering firm. All of them are professionally qualified engineers, except for the financial director who is a chartered accountant. All are very intelligent people. During the first coaching session, I asked each one a couple of questions—the same ones that Alfonzo Lopez had asked me a couple of weeks before when he visited me.

Suppose you are faced with a very important personal decision to make, and you only have two hours in which to make it, what conditions would you seek out? Where would you want to go in order to evaluate most effectively? What state of mind would you want to be in?

Without exception the answers were down the line of "a quiet and peaceful place; somewhere where I can think without interference. My mind must be clear and peaceful." Anger and urgency can so easily destroy such conditions.

Don't fool yourself by thinking that you are only angry when you shout, rant and rave. There is such a thing as 'silent' anger, where you are upset inside, but it does not necessarily show that much on the outside. Such a state can also block you from effective 'Edo'. In fact, having an unresolved grudge against someone is simply another form of anger. Such unresolved negative feelings towards someone will make it more difficult to judge the actions of that person objectively—you think you can, but you can't. I am really referring here to emotional maturity.

I recorded an incident in my journal where we had a specific challenge with a leader who managed a large project in a well-known organization. The team had to deliver on a very important project, but there wasn't unity among the team members. A friend asked my partner and me to come in and assist. After the brief, we even offered some free time, which they gladly accepted, as budgets were tight. The leader came late, left, then came back again but could only stay for a certain period. The free time was being squandered. Then the leader wanted to cancel and re-schedule. She told my partner and me to discuss between ourselves whether we were willing to come back again, but if we were not willing to come back for more free time the relationship had to end. It felt like a slap in the face. I was getting angry fast! My partner and I walked out and in so-called 'controlled' anger decided that was it! We wanted to go back and end the relationship. It really seemed like a very reasonable and fair thing to 'do'. But, maturity prevailed. We decided to 'evaluate' just a little bit longer. We realized that the reputation of our friend who confidently recommended us was at stake and that the team needed us, because the leader seemed possibly to be one of the major obstacles. We rose above immaturity and pride and walked back into the conference room with our decision, only to be asked fairly assertively by the leader to leave as she was now having a discussion with her team. This was another test for us to move away from our mature decision, but we stuck to our guns and on the way out my partner said, "We have decided we are willing to come back, and we will do it for free." We walked out and knew the group would be fair. Shortly afterwards, the leader came out and sincerely thanked us for our agreement. The group wanted us back. In fact, we heard after the incident that when we entered they were debating whether or not they should offer to pay us. When we interrupted and told them what our decision was, they were very impressed with the way we handled the situation.

After the incident, we thought for a moment that if only we didn't enter the room so quickly we might have been paid for the next round, but we knew we had done the right thing. Our integrity was unquestionable, and the leader respected us more than before. My partner suggested we would be blessed in other ways, which prediction came true. Later that day, more business came in from another customer and following our next free intervention we did more work for the client and we were paid for it. During the next couple of weeks, I could also see how the leader matured. She read *The CEO Leadership Handbook* and sincerely tried to apply the principles. Why did she even consider reading the book and then applying the principles? She respected us! Why could she respect us? Because in this instance we applied 'Edo' effectively. Subsequently, she asked us to come in again for another critical facilitation session.

If you want to be a great leader, you must ensure that you learn to control your emotions so that your state of mind is such that you can 'Edo' effectively.

A while back, we decided to do some alterations to our office upstairs while away on holiday. My PA oversaw it all. Her husband was out of work so it was suggested that he did the sanding and painting, for which we would compensate him. The hope was also that all would be complete by the time we got back. Well, it wasn't, not nearly! Upon our return, I evaluated the work that had already been done. The list of negatives just grew and grew, which seems to be a universal result of any building job. I became concerned about having to address a friend about the negatives. I kept saying to myself that you should never give such a job to someone you know. I asked myself why we always make the same mistake of asking a friend, with all the right intentions. On top of this, he promised to come in early on the day we got back. He only arrived about midday. Fortunately, just before I went upstairs to discuss the job, I decided to fall back to simplicity—first hear the other side of the story; do not make a judgment yet. In other words, 'evaluate' the job with the other party present and do not go into 'do' mode yet. I asked him to explain how things went and how he saw it going forward. As he explained, most of my concerns faded away like mist before the sun. The context changed. I made a note in my journal as follows:

"What is the simple universal principle? Do not make a judgment [what to do] about any situation involving others until you have heard their side of the story."

Selfish desires

Selfish desires or aspirations can also be an obstacle to confident and effective 'Edo'. If life is just about you and your personal ambitions, you will battle to make decisions for the good of the organization or other people. Somewhere down the line, there will be a clash of aspirations and your decision will have a negative impact on the organization or person in question. I believe what our nation really questioned when it came to Thabo Mbeki's decisions about Jacob Zuma's future was what desires or aspirations drove the decision. Some believed they were of a selfish nature, others didn't, and others didn't know what to think.

Other

Other traps that make 'Edo' more difficult could be pride (I know it all); low self-esteem; constant worrying; fear; guilt and anxiety.

Finally, watch out for the trap of doing, doing and doing without evaluating properly, and watch out for the trap of evaluating, evaluating and evaluating without ever doing—analysis paralysis. You also have to remember that in some situations you cannot assemble all the facts, yet you have to make a decision. Sizwe Nxasana, the CEO of First Rand Bank, explains, "We must accept as leaders that we cannot wait until we have all the facts and information before we make a decision. It is important for you to listen, debate, discuss and collect information to the extent that you can, and remember to use your intuition all the time ... You have got to make a decision. And ask if at the time you made that decision with all the facts that were in front of you, were you acting in the interest of your organization and did you really believe that the decision you took was the best one given the information and facts before you?" Of course, this principle could easily apply in a personal situation as well.

I encourage you to consciously become aware of and fight against those obstacles or traps that you can potentially fall into that impact negatively on your ability to 'Edo' (evaluate and do) effectively and with confidence.

'Edo' and people interaction

I have pondered for a long time what universal principles are most critical to 'Edo' when it comes to people interaction and building trust in relationships. I am starting to believe that treating others as you want to be treated is certainly one of them: do to others what you would want done to you. I simply call it the Do-Done principle. The other critical universal principle is 'personal standards'—to be discussed later.

Do-Done principle

Imagine the following situations:

Situation 1—You drive down the road in a hurry, as usual. You have an urgent meeting to attend. If all goes well, you may just make it on time. But, true to form the green light switches over to orange and the car in front of you obediently slows down and stops. You know that if it were you, you would have taken a small chance and driven on. How would you feel at this stage—frustrated, angry, upset? This is not all. The light turns green again and the driver in front of you stalls his car. How do you feel now? How do you act? And then you see in the back window a sign indicating the driver is in training. How do you feel now? How do you act? It is probably not enough to calm you down totally, is it?

Situation 2—You are on holiday, which is the only time of year you are able to catch up on your yearly reading quota. You are engrossed in a magnificent book! Your five-year-old son storms into your room where you are comfortably lying on the bed. He wants to swim in the communal pool. You don't like swimming and he is just learning to swim. How do you feel? How do you act?

Situation 3—You are relaxing with a couple of friends, chatting about everything and anything that is not of real importance. Everyone is in a casual mood. Suddenly, someone opens a discussion on another person who all of you believe is a little 'strange'. You know, that kind of person who is just difficult to get a handle on; someone with strange mannerisms; someone with a low EQ; someone who overstays their welcome; who easily steps into your personal space; who just manages to drain most people's energy levels; someone who you try to avoid at a social gathering. Your friends start laughing as this person is discussed openly. How do you feel? How do you act?

The above three situations are real. They happen to all of us at some point in time, in some form or another. How would a person of great character or a great leader react in such situations? I think great leaders instinctively apply the Do-Done principle.

Do-Done application

When you 'Edo' situations that involve proactively building relationships with people, this guideline will be universally valuable. It is not the be all and end all but, if you follow the Do-Done principle, I make you a promise that your 'Edo' process will be more effective and you will become better at building proactive, trusting relationships with people. You will also have a clear conscience when you go to bed at night. When you treat others differently from how you want to be treated, you start polluting your conscience—you feel guilty, which in turn affects your 'Edo' ability.

Back to the above situations:

Situation 1—You are the young person behind the steering wheel in the middle of your first lesson on a real public road. You accidentally stall the car. How would you like the person behind you to act towards you? Think about it. What action would impress you most if done by the driver behind you? Would you simply expect patience and understanding? Would you appreciate and be impressed with an understanding smile? Would you be impressed with a universal 'thumbs up' signal? What a difference the acceptance of 'do to others what you would want done to you' principle can have on your behaviour.

Situation 2—You are the five-year-old boy who has just learned to swim. When you are in that pool, you receive praise, and it is just so much fun. What do you want your father to do when you ask him to take you for a swim? Do you want him to say, "Not now!"? Do you want him to ignore you? Do you want him to give you half of his attention? Do you want him to say he will take you in five minutes? Just think what you would want your father to say and do and you will 'Edo' more effectively.

Situation 3—You are the person who is not present with those whom you consider to be your friends. Do you want them to discuss you openly in a mocking manner? Would you want everyone to join in the discussion? Would you want someone to remain silent to soothe his/her conscience with the thought of "At least I didn't join in"? Would you want someone to assertively but politely recommend they don't speak about other people in their absence? In fact, would you be most impressed if someone mentioned something positive about you and in that way changed the discussion to a positive one?

In the last minute of my recent interview with Dr Stephen R. Covey, I asked him to give our listeners/viewers some final counsel. He said this: "Realize that you have four parts to your nature: Body—assume you had a heart attack, now exercise and eat accordingly; Mind—assume the half life of your profession is two or three years, now prepare accordingly; Heart—assume everything you say about another person they can hear, now speak accordingly; Spirit—assume you had a one-on-one visit with your creator every three months, now live accordingly." Great advice!

Consider any possible people interaction situation and the effect that the Do-Done principle can have on it. Have you had an argument or fairly negative interaction with your partner recently? If so, then evaluate the situation by measuring it against the Do-Done principle (do to others what you would want done to you). The chances are that if you were in your partner's shoes you would want him or her to apologize, or you would be very impressed if he or she came to you and asked to once again hear your side of the situation without interruption. You would be somewhat impressed if he or she apologized for yelling at you, and for losing his or her temper. Using the Do-Done principle as an 'Edo' tool immediately brings clarity and simplicity to what seemed to be a very complicated situation, especially if your standard in this instance is to be an understanding, loving partner.

This morning I committed to washing the dishes—only happens on holiday as dishwashers are not freely available. My wife left the apartment to visit her uncle. I became so engrossed with writing that I totally forgot about the dishes. When Melissa got back in time to prepare lunch, the dishes were not done. She had to start preparing in a small kitchen full of dirty dishes. In fact, she started washing the dishes. I did not live up to the Do-Done standard, so I was in the dog box. But, fortunately it was possible to rectify the situation by applying the same principle. I evaluated against the Do-Done standard—if I was in Melissa's shoes, what would I want my husband to do? First of all, I was clear on my standard of wanting to be a loving and understanding husband. Then I asked myself if I would want him to come down and humbly apologize and then help further where he could? Yes, and this is what I did. It worked!

Do-Done and standards

It is humanly impossible to perform above those standards that we truly believe in and value most. This is not simply an ethics statement, but a universal law that governs the performance of every human being.

It is not possible to perform above our believed (real) standards in life; in other words, that which you truly believe in, in your heart and mind. It is human to perform below our standards at times, but it is impossible to continually or as a matter of course perform above them. In other words, it does not help to express or agree verbally to a standard simply because it's what the boss wants to hear or because it will please the other party. You may be able to hide the fact that you don't really believe in the standard, but it will catch up with you sooner or later.

Standards in this context include all those desires, expectations, principles, objectives and goals we sincerely believe in, and so value most. There are in fact two kinds of valued standards:

1) Standards of behaviour—e.g. professionalism and integrity.
2) Standards of performance—e.g. sales targets and productivity levels.

We perform according to our imposed and ultimately, self-imposed, limitations and standards.

I have had many people challenge this law of: It is humanly impossible to perform above those standards that we truly believe and value most. They feel that it is possible to set a specific standard like sales targets, actually believe within yourself that the standard is too high, and then achieve or exceed it. Yes, there may be moments or exceptional circumstances where this happens. However, if it happens that you aim for a standard that you don't believe is possible to reach, and you reach or exceed it, you yourself will probably not be the reason behind the achievement. It may happen because of someone else's contribution, someone who believed it was possible. However, what may also have happened before you reached or exceeded the standard is that your believability levels were raised somewhere along the way. Perhaps you set a target for R1 million in sales by the end of December and you expected to be at R800,000 by October, but after reviewing your October figures you realize you are on R850,000. What happens to your believability levels? You raise them! You start believing that it is possible to reach or even exceed the R1 million mark.

When it comes to standards of performance it may be easier to measure whether or not one has achieved or exceeded them. In other words, it is easy to see whether you accomplished your sales targets. But, when it comes to standards of behaviour it becomes more difficult. How do you measure whether a leader performs below or above the standard of honesty, or the standard of professionalism? This is why organizations, in general, battle to live up to their standards of behaviour. Often they struggle to even define them clearly.

Humankind has been endowed with the gift of choice. So many of us take this for granted. Few of us measure the price we have to pay when we take this gift lightly. Because of this gift, you ultimately have to choose what valued standards (values) you want to live by, and these standards are inseparably connected with your ability to act with confidence. When you do not act in line with those values that you know in your heart are right, you in effect follow weaker or lower standards. Your ability to see situations in context is limited, which in turn leads to incorrect decisions and ultimately a decrease in confidence. This is why it can be very difficult to work for an organization where the value system—defined or not—is not aligned with your own, especially when you are very clear about your own standards. In fact, it could be just as difficult for people who set high standards of performance for themselves to work in an organization or division that just plods along. Such a misalignment may result in them becoming more visible and being raised to positions of increased authority. It may also result in them being seen as a threat by others in power, resulting in life being made difficult for them. They may also become frustrated and leave.

As mentioned earlier, it is humanly possible to perform below the level of your valued standards in life. But when you fail you can mostly try again and succeed. However, if in the first instance your standards are low and simply convenient, then it becomes impossible to reach any real heights of character. Your standards, like goals should stretch you.

Valued standards are a personal issue, a matter of personal choice. They determine your horizons and your potential. To move towards your leadership destiny with more confidence you have to know the answer to the following question: What do I value most in life?

If you have not yet taken time out to answer this question sincerely, I suggest you do it soon! Use the old 'death bed' trick by imagining you are on your death bed with your child/children by your side. Now give them advice on what life is about; what really matters in life; what real happiness is; what you believe they should value most in their lives.

In spite of the modern tendency to rationalize high moral and other more traditional values, all of us have a profound admiration for those individuals who do the right thing no matter what the cost; who stand up for their values no matter what the potential repercussions. This is the reason why individuals and organizations that strive after excellence always try to live by a set of high valued standards of behaviour such as honesty, integrity, loyalty, unity, knowledge, diligence and fairness.

Sizwe Nxasana says it this way: "It is important to create a sense of values in an organization. It is important for people to have a common understanding of what everybody is trying to do and which direction the organization is trying to head towards. If you create that kind of condition, it becomes easy for people to relate to the organization; it becomes easy for an organization, even today with the advent of regulations and laws, to operate in an environment where the subtle values underpin and form the foundation and basis for what we are doing in an organization."

A couple of years ago, I interviewed General Robert C. Oaks. He was one of the top generals in the US Air Force; someone who not only had his own chauffeur but his own Air Force jet in which he moved around. The budget he was responsible for was probably larger than the South African government's budget. I heard he was driving up to Tzaneen alone, so I asked to travel with him in order to interview him. I remember how impressed I was with how he treated the people around him, such as the woman at the toll gate or the petrol attendant. He was so friendly to them and treated them as important individuals in the way he greeted them, or the way he said good-bye.

In 1976, when he was still a colonel in the United States Air Force, he was a member of the Incidents at Sea negotiating team. They were guests at a dinner hosted by the Leningrad Naval District. About 50 senior officers of the Soviet Union and the United States were present as the host led the group in toasts before dinner. They stood for the first toast and raised their glasses, most of which were filled with Russian vodka. Colonel Oaks had pink lemonade in his glass, which was immediately noticed by the admiral leading the toast. He stopped and demanded that Colonel Oaks fill his glass with vodka, stating that he would not proceed until he had done so. Colonel Oaks declined, explaining that he was happy with what he had in his glass. A significant tension began to build, and even his own team members, most of whom were senior to him, were growing uneasy over the impasse. Colonel Oaks' Soviet escort hissed in his ear, "Fill your glass with vodka!"

Colonel Oaks uttered the shortest prayer of his life: "God help me!"

Within seconds, the Soviet interpreter, an army captain with whom he had previously discussed religion, whispered to the host admiral, "It is because of his religion."

The admiral nodded his head, the tension immediately diffused, and the programme moved on.

Years before this incident, Colonel Oaks had decided that he valued the standard of not drinking alcohol. Even in such a challenging situation, he remained true to his standard. You may think that his persistence in this case pushed the limits, and that with so many of his seniors present such an action would have harmed his career. Well, it didn't. He went on to become a four-star general and leader of tens of thousands of people in various fields of life. Interestingly, though, he believes that, in spite of a lifelong career studying leadership, the basis of all his leadership ability was the teachings of his mother. Great leaders are committed to universal standards that can be taught to a child. Sizwe Nxasana told me that when the chips are down and he is facing a very difficult position he always wonders what his mother would have told him about that particular situation and invariably he gets an answer.

Ian Cockerill is the CEO of Gold Fields Ltd, one of the largest gold mining companies in the world. With his team, they managed to overcome the attempted takeover by Harmony Gold a couple of years ago. You may remember how the whole story dominated business headlines for months. Ian was also awarded the title of Leading Manager—end 2007. What does he say about valued standards of behaviour, or values?

"Foundation values permeate your whole existence ... Core principles that I grew up with and were handed down to me by my parents, I have tried to bring through to my business life."

On a personal note, I was touched by this experience of Oaks, as many years ago I set the same standard of not drinking alcohol in my life. After school, I chose to go to the South African Police Force for four years rather than attend the army for two. Following my five or so months of college training, I was drafted to the Radio Control Unit. I could not understand why I had to go and work with radios after all the training. Little did I know that this division was in fact the Flying Squad, where one supposedly drove around in faster cars, chasing through the streets of Pretoria and generally arriving on the scene before the common police vans. My fellow college colleagues were jealous of where I was going. Well, I wasn't there for too long when it was announced that new recruits would undergo their initiation, which took the form of a shift braai where the newcomers to that specific shift had to drink alcohol until they dropped. I recall there were four of us and each one decided this was nonsense—we simply would not succumb to the pressure. The day arrived and, as a young man surrounded by tough, bearded cops, I was really nervous. You see, I knew that no matter what happened I would not drink! I was not sure how committed the other three chaps were to the standard we had set, but I was as committed as could be. Guess what happened on the day? Eventually, each one of the others succumbed to the pressure. They decided to drink just this time to get it over with and it did not take long before they were rolling around in the mud. I insisted I would not drink. Rumours went around that they would force me. It wasn't easy, but I hung in there. Not much later, some of the older men came to me in secret and explained how much they admired me for sticking to my standard. You see, alcohol can bring out the worst in someone, but it often brings out honest feelings as well. Later, they tried to get me to be the barman, but I wasn't too great at that.

Back to the Do-Done principle. In some life situations, your Do-Done answer may clash with your personal standards, which could pose a problem. In such a case, you may have to evaluate more before deciding what to do. I believe in some exceptional situations, however, you may have to go with the Do-Done answer and raise your personal standard. But, in other situations, you will have to lean towards your personal standards. Consider the story of General Oaks. If he had not decided to live by a certain standard in his life, and then applied the Do-Done principle during that situation, he probably would have acted differently. He would have drunk the vodka because, if he was in the shoes of the admiral, he would have wanted the American officer to drink the vodka. But, applying Do-Done against his personal standard led to his 'doing' what he did.

The Thabo Mbeki and Jacob Zuma situation that occurred in 2005 also illustrates the importance of linking Do-Done with personal standards. After a judge declared that Jacob Zuma was implicated as having had a corrupt relationship with a well-known businessman, what was Thabo Mbeki to 'do'? If he used the Do-Done principle, he may have asked the following question: If I were Zuma, how would I want the president of the country to treat me? Here comes the snag. I may not want him to fire me. Oops! The Do-Done principle does not work for me at this stage of the process. But, what standards am I measuring this situation against? I want a corruption-free government, or at least one that is perceived that way. I want leaders with high ethics and morals, especially those who drive the moral regeneration programmes. Now, from this base I can work backwards again. The standard of not allowing corruption must be upheld. This is a given and a non-negotiable. But, what I would at least want from the president of the country would be to be treated with respect and dignity. I would want the president not to use the situation for selfish personal gain but to simply do what is right for the right reasons, and so on.

Imagine a situation where your child does not do his agreed upon chores for pocket money. If you evaluate the situation by using the Do-Done principle only, it would once again fail. If I were my son, what would I want done to me? Of course I would want my father to feel sorry for me and give me my pocket money anyway. But, we set a standard that for certain tasks a certain amount would be paid. We also live a standard in our home of being fair. We want our children to learn that you have to work hard in life for what you want and to be successful.

Have another look at the first situation earlier on in the chapter where the learner driver's car stalls. If you do not have any set standard in your mind and heart of how a good citizen should act, you will battle to come up with a reasonable Do-Done standard. It will be easier for you to default towards following the lower standard of anger or frustration.

Also have a look at the second situation where your child interrupts your reading activity. Once again link the answer to your standard that you have set for yourself as a father. Perhaps your standard is that you never want your child to feel that anything in life is more important to you. In this case, you would probably put the book down immediately and head off to the swimming pool. However, add to this standard that you also want to teach the principle that as an only child he has to learn to keep himself busy at times and that mom and dad cannot always play with him at the drop of a hat, even though there is nothing more important to mom and dad than he is. What will you do in this case? Maybe you will opt for taking him in five minutes, after a clear explanation? If you follow the Do-Done standard but you have a standard or belief that children are there to be seen and not heard, how will you act? The answer is obvious.

If you want to be a great leader, learn to set standards for yourself, your family, your team or your organization, together, and keep lifting those standards—raising the bar! Ian Cockerill explains that when they come up with a strategy and actions following rigorous debate and discussions, they make sure it is "rational, sensible, practical and it can be done, yet it has the relevant amount of stretch in so that they continually raise the bar."

Stretching your people may at times result in you not being popular in the short term, but you will be respected in the long term, and more often than not even in the short term. It is more important to be respected than to be liked!

Remember, most of the time relationships go wrong because we did not in the first instance live up to the Do-Done standard. It therefore requires the same standard to get things back on track—TiLi!

Lessons learned

Ultimately, how you evaluate and how you 'do' is what wisdom is all about. So, if you want to reach your destiny of being a greater leader, you need to learn to 'Edo' effectively with confidence. In order to do this, you need to avoid or learn to manage all obstacles that stand in your way. Simple, isn't it? No one said it would be easy though—TiLi!

"The difference between a great and a mediocre leader is often determined by the degree of simplicity with which he or she views life"

'Edo' factor: All situations in life consist of only two universal actions—evaluate and do.

Obstacles to confident and effective 'Edo' include: ignorance; pressure to act quickly; urgency; anger; selfish desires; pride; 'I know it all' attitude; low self-esteem; constant worrying; fear; guilt; anxiety; and so on.

Do-Done: "Do to others as you would want done to you."

It is humanly impossible to perform above those standards that we truly believe and value most.

Measure the Do-Done principle against your personal standards.

CHAPTER THREE

'EDO' AND MOVEMENT

"Life is all about movement"

The Law of Movement

I often ask a group of people that I am addressing if they agree with the following statement: Life is all about movement.

Of course they mostly agree, following which I ask them why they agree. They respond that life is about constant change (movement), development (movement) and growth (movement). I then jokingly ask them all to stop moving, to freeze, which they obediently do. Why don't you do the same for a moment?

Now, let us discuss whether or not you did in fact stop moving. The answer is of course no. You had to continue breathing, the blood in your veins continued to flow, and your heart continued pumping. Life is all about movement. Without movement you die!

Instinctively, you also want to breathe life into lifeless situations. You always want to move from an existing situation to a better one. Even if you want to maintain a successful situation, you still have to keep moving or else the situation may cease being successful. You want to move ahead in your career; you want to move forward in important relationships; you want to move forward intellectually; and you want to move forward in your health.

A major break-through in striving towards your leadership destiny is understanding the next universal law that great leaders apply subconsciously—the Law of Movement. In the context of the 'Edo' factor, to 'do' is to move; to understand and believe in the Law of Movement is to 'do' profitably and depend less on luck and fate. The law will help you understand what universal elements must be in place for successful 'doing'. And, by implication, you would have to evaluate the same elements to ensure they are in place before 'doing'.

The universal Law of Movement states the following: All movement in life is governed by integration of motivation, direction and supporting structure.

Earlier on in the book, I asked you if it was possible that all situations in life can consist of only two universal actions, namely 'evaluate' and 'do'. I now ask you if it is actually possible that all movement that you deal with in life can consist of only three over-arching elements or components. Yes, it is! All movement in life is governed by the integration or even alignment of these three universal elements. In other words, for anything to move, or to be positioned from one point to another, the elements of motivation, direction and structure are essential, a given.

By understanding the universal governing elements or ingredients of all movement in life, you will make a quantum leap in understanding how to move yourself, other people, situations and even organizations towards your and their destinies. In other words, you will become a greater leader!

Motivation

Motivation is the driving element of movement. It is the energy needed for anything to move. Without motivation (reason, motive, purpose, desire, aspiration, energy) of some kind, nothing will move at all. The quality of motivation becomes a critical success factor with regard to successful living. This is why the age-old advice to the question of what career you should follow is always to do what you love most. When you 'evaluate' what to 'do' with your future, you have to consider your talents and interests if you want to not only become successful but also happy.

The term we use to describe the essence of human motivation is positive aspirations. When people passionately and maturely want things to happen—aspire towards something—they happen! Ever heard of the phrase: Where there is a will, there is a way? Motivation and positive aspirations are therefore synonymous. In 1994, the various political leaders in South Africa were motivated enough to move the country forward profitably—they passionately shared the positive aspiration of a peaceful transition.

Direction

Direction is the second element and is inseparably connected with motivation or your aspirations.

Motivation without direction is senseless. It would be the same as wanting (desiring, aspiring) to become a great leader without following a plan for improvement; or to really want to go on holiday but not deciding where and how you will get there. Motivation cannot exist without direction. It is how we accomplish our aspirations. Yet, some individuals go through life without committing to clear directions, goals, or simple actions of how they will reach their motives or aspirations. They want something—a position, a successful business—but they don't constructively plan and decide on a specific direction.

From a life context, everything we do has directional meaning. We use terms such as mission, vision, strategy, plans, objectives and goals. All these are directional issues in one form or another.

From the perspective of the basic movement model, motivation and direction are essential ingredients of all movement towards a 'great leadership' destiny.

Structure

Structure is the third basic element of universal movement. Structure in the context of the model refers to resources, facilities, systems, procedures or an organization needed to give substance to aspirations and direction. In other words, structure is a universal principle without which aspirations and direction cannot take place.

In profitable movement, structure is designed to assist aspirations and direction, not the other way around. All plans are based on aspirations, coupled with directional strategy. Structure is used to carry out the plans. If the structure is not in place, then it must be created, or the lack of it would result in unsuccessful 'doing' (movement). Structure always serves aspirations in a profitable and happy environment. The quality of motivation, clarity of direction and relevance of structure become essential factors in movement towards a successful destiny.

When I am in the presence of leaders who need to be convinced of the reality of the Law of Movement, I illustrate it as follows.

I walk up to one of the leaders in the room, shake his hand and walk back to my original spot. I then ask the group if I moved, which of course I did. We then analyse whether, in this simple act, the Law of Movement holds true. Did I have a motive/reason/purpose for moving? Yes, it was to illustrate some point or it was simply to greet the person. Did I have a direction? Yes. What structure did I use? My legs and feet, the carpet, etc. We then agree that even in the simple act of walking we apply the Law of Movement, without consciously knowing it.

To prove that all three components of the law must be present, I say out loud to the group that it is my intention to illustrate something to them by walking over to so and so. I then remain static until it becomes uncomfortably quiet in the room and attendees even start sniggering. I ask them what is wrong. The answer—"You didn't move."

I then respond by asking if I had a motive, reason or purpose to move, to which they answer 'yes'. I then ask if I had a direction, to which they once again answer 'yes'.

"What was missing?" I ask them. They usually answer clearly that structure—legs, feet, etc.—didn't do its part. So, without one of the components, movement does not occur. Viewed from another angle, two out of the three components simply won't do if you want to move effectively towards your destiny!

Too many great concepts or ideas die a slow death because the person driving them could not mobilize the necessary structure or resources. There is motivation and even confidence in how they would go about marketing the product or invention, in other words direction, but when it comes to raising capital to realize the idea they fail. In some cases, they manage to raise some structure but they start off with irrelevant structure—lovely, but unnecessary, offices with more than they need. Stephen Saad, founder and CEO of the very successful Aspen Pharmaceutical giant says it this way: "I have seen so many small businesses fail because people want to go straight into a fancy office and have a big car and do all the things that supposedly come with running your own business. That can wait! There will be a time for that! First make sure your business is successful, because most businesses fail in those first few years. If you can get over those first few years, then you will be successful. Yes, you will not be able to play golf every Saturday … but those are some of the sacrifices you might have to make to become successful in your business."

The challenge of needing to access structure exists at all levels. One of Russell Loubser's greatest challenges as a leader for nine years at the JSE was realizing the magnitude of the change that had to take place. Russell took the first few months to analyze fully what had to happen. He then realized that part of the challenge was that they had no money to effect the change; in other words, they lacked structure, according to the Law of Movement.

We have all heard the stories of how McDonalds or Kentucky Fried Chicken came about—how the originator walked from restaurant to restaurant with his recipe until eventually he found a willing buyer. What drove him to persevere? First of all, a passionate desire or aspiration—high motivation—but he also instinctively realized that without structure his concept would die—stop moving.

I love the story of how Discovery Health was born. In the late 1980s, Adrian Gore was a young man in his late twenties working for another large corporate in an industry that was in crisis. He had the idea to launch a product to combat some of the challenges, which he did. It was very successful because the product was good and there was a huge demand for it. He approached a financial institution with the idea of forming a company with an American-type style—specialist, focused, with a different ethos. They liked the idea and agreed to inject the seed capital into it—R10 million. In March 1992, he began with a desk, a chair and a rented office. That's how Discovery began. Even today, when he pulls out the original business plan, there is not one number in it. The proposal or plan is all about philosophy, about building a company that would feel different; the business objectives and intent were correct. Only several months later did they put together important figures, like return on capital, etc. This story illustrates perfectly what the role of structure should be, namely to serve aspirations and directions. This philosophy has infiltrated the business. You see, the leader instinctively feels and acts upon the universal way of doing things.

Gore believes, for example, that, "As a leader you have to be authentic; you have to have a real purpose [motivation], or else people see through you ... People are not motivated by just success or money. If they believe they are in an organization that has a noble purpose [aligning aspirations], they will push harder; they will be motivated. I think any great leader has to do that."

Universal application

The power and authority of the basic movement law or process can best be appreciated when you try to disprove it! Try to visualize any kind of movement—of people, ideas, organizations, actions, things and animals—that is not governed by these three universal principles. You will find that this universal process governs all movement, whether you acknowledge it or not. The flying bird is dependent on the three elements: motivation (whatever drives the bird to fly—hungry chicks), direction (or else the bird would be standing still, not moving—wherever the food was before), and structure (in the case of the bird, it needs a body, feathers, sky, etc.).

As you read this book, you are governed by these three elements. You are motivated to read the book (whatever the motivation may be, e.g. wanting to increase your confidence to move towards your own 'great leadership' destiny); direction (to read the book—the very act of reading denotes directional meaning consisting of desires, objectives and disciplines); and structure (the actual book, a body, physical senses, a place to sit and read, light, reading spectacles, etc. in order to be able to read).

You can relate the basic movement process to every conceivable situation in life. The organization for which you work exists because this law is in force! Somewhere along the line some motive—desire or need—in the marketplace resulted in a decision to follow a direction that would satisfy the motive (desire, need), followed by the mobilization of some physical structures—office building, computers, etc.

If you want to be successful in moving yourself, a team, a company, a country or any situation, you must understand and believe the Law of Movement, as you do the Law of Gravity—TiLi!

Nothing in life moves without some motive, or something motivating it, to move. Test this universal truth on yourself. You yourself need a motive (reason) to move, and if you are passionately committed to the motive, you will move with energy, commitment, dedication and absolute accountability. Every single day of your life you are driven by motives that are strong enough to move you. You get out of bed for a reason. That reason (motive) could simply be going to work to have the means to pay the bills, or it could be that you want to go out there and make a difference in people's lives, probably resulting in higher motivation.

Profitable movement process

It is, however, critical to remember that nothing in life can move profitably or successfully in isolation! It is impossible for an individual in his or her marriage or career, or for a department, company, country or any entity to move forward successfully or profitably, alone! In your career, there are important stakeholders with whom you should align (integrate)—staff, boss, peers, customers, etc. A company should integrate or align with customers, staff, community, government and shareholders. Profitable movement is not possible without the concept of integration and alignment. In short, you will not and cannot be a great leader in isolation and without an attitude of integration—TiLi!

A person or country that finds itself in the same position as South Africa (apartheid era), Zimbabwe (current Mugabe era), Iraq (Saddam era), Germany (Hitler era), the Soviet Union (communist era), Enron, Fidentia and so on, will not move profitably while ignoring or even misreading the aspirations of key stakeholders. When any person starts thinking that he or she can move forward profitably in isolation, or without integrating with essential stakeholders, the result will eventually be failure. Unfortunately, before that happens, many stakeholders will suffer and will not obtain benefit from the movement.

Great leaders adopt an integrative style in the process of arriving at the universal components of movement.

Alan Woolfson, former MD of what used to be Charter Life Insurance, explains a motive behind following the integrative and profitable movement process in the corporate environment well.

"You know if you are a leader who is right 80 per cent of the time, you can afford to be a dictatorial leader. The fact that it would be hard to retain bright people working under these circumstances is an issue, but most of the decisions made would be right. But with the incredible complexity of our work environment, a leader's decisions would probably be right about 50 per cent of the time. So, you can up that percentage by getting input from other people. The main thing is to get as much input as possible before making a decision, pushing up your 'hit rate' as high as possible."

Louisa Mojela, the CEO of Wiphold, put it this way when I interviewed her several years ago, "Good leadership, I believe, needs to be integrated. Yes, there has to be a leader, but you always have to encompass your colleagues and make sure that no one is lagging behind with what the strategy of the company is."

To move profitably in any given situation, you must understand who the important stakeholders are, and then integrate with their positive aspirations (motivation), directions, and structures, or ensure that they can integrate with yours.

Nelson Mandela is a great example of the universal principle of positive aspiration integration in order to create motivation. During the Rugby World Cup that was played in South Africa in 1995, he arrived at the opening game with a green number 6 Springbok pullover. That single, masterful act went a long way in integrating the positive and personal aspirations of South Africans from vastly different poles.

Rugby is the darling sport of most Afrikaners, and support for rugby among black South Africans was minimal. That act by the president of a very diverse, brittle, sensitive nation, following the first democratic elections in 1994, sparked off a World Cup competition that exploded into an event that unified South Africa as never before, and perhaps never again. The aspiration to win the World Cup transcended all other aspirations and the victory by the Springboks was the crowning moment and sweet taste of what it feels like when a nation is fully integrated in the process towards, and the accomplishment of, an aspiration.

Unfortunately, you cannot realistically integrate with all stakeholders all the time! For this reason, a fourth principle is added to the profitable movement process—'Becoming an adjustor'.

Becoming an adjustor

There is always a price to be paid for not complying with the integration of positive aspirations, direction and structure. Profitable movement is stifled in some way or another. Why do marriages come to an end? At the risk of over simplifying it, the answer lies in the movement and profitable movement process. The husband and wife start aspiring towards different things, or they start disagreeing on the directions needed to get to their aspirations. In so many cases, the lack of structures (resources, money) or even the surplus of structures, leads to disharmony and movement in different directions. If such a situation is not remedied quickly, the cost factor increases. In time, it becomes so heavy that the couple decides to adjust the situation—live separate lives or get a divorce.

If an organization cannot integrate with the positive career aspirations of a good staff member, the cost could be that of losing the individual to the competition, which leads to the cost of having to retrain a new employee, in which period the department may lose focus on its direction for a while, which once again has obvious costs attached to it. If your organization cannot integrate with the Employment Equity aspirations of the government, the cost could be a financial penalty of sorts.

To become an adjustor means you have to learn to act tough or implement difficult actions. Many people are not willing to follow tough or hard steps to get their own or someone else's situation or even life back on course. I have seen this in families where a child is a drug addict and eventually stops integrating with the aspirations, directions and structures of the family. For years, the family tries to get back to the profitable movement process, but this one member of the family just continues to ignore and move against the family's aspirations. Such cases more often than not require adjustment—tough love, even to the point of banning the addicted family member from entering the house or allowing the law to take its course. But, the family just can't do this! What happens? The cost factor just gets heavier and heavier and the effects on the entire family are devastating.

As you grow in your ability to understand and monitor the profitable movement process, you develop sensitivity to critical indicators that you or those around you are not complying with the elements of the process. If you have the courage to be an adjustor, you will not shy away from confronting threats to performance or profitable movement. These threats are often ignored or missed because of the fear of having to act tough and they show in abstract ways before they show in more obvious ways. Examples are moments of contention, silent treatment, backstabbing, disloyalty, lack of enthusiasm and lack of innovation. A great leader can look into someone's eyes and sense that the person is not in aspiration mode, but rather stuck in a negative frame of mind—a destructive one.

To be a great leader, you require an adjustor attitude, so that deviations from aspirations and directions can be picked up before they result in crisis situations.

Adjusting examples

Challenging staff member: You may have a staff member with whom you are not able to integrate. The feeling that the relationship is not moving profitably is tangible. Because of this, there is a cost factor. The cost may be miscommunication between yourself and the individual, negativity, a loss of productivity, mistrust, a bad influence on other staff and ultimately unsatisfactory performance.

You could live with this cost and while doing so try your utmost to follow the universal process to integrate. As the cost adds up, you will arrive at the crucial point of having to adjust. In other words, you would have to act in a way that is essentially contrary to the principles of the integration process, with the intention of returning to it as soon as possible.

You know in which ways you could adjust. They range from disciplinary hearings to transferring him or her to some remote area in the world. But adjusting also has a cost attached to it. It could vary from your time and energy to financial implications. You need to weigh up (evaluate) the cost factor and the cost of adjusting, and then 'do'.

Many great leaders fail in this area of profitable movement. They pass the pivotal point—the crucial crossover between evaluating and doing. The cost factor increases exponentially when the pivotal point is passed, and depending on the critical nature of the position that the 'problem child' holds, the company could end up in serious difficulties.

Adjustment strategies can be very difficult. The situation that you have to adjust could be sensitive. It may involve someone who has been a friend for years. It may be an individual whom you used to work for in the past, and now he or she reports to you. It may even be someone that you recruited and have been backing or sponsoring, and your adjustment strategy in effect will be an admission of error in judgment on your part. In fact, the person towards whom you should be acting tough may be a family member. These are some of the many reasons why it is easy to avoid or procrastinate adjusting actions.

Another reason for falling into the trap of not adjusting is that it is perceived to be sudden and traumatic, even though the cost factor may have added up slowly over a long period of time. It reminds me of the frog-in-water syndrome. Place a frog in cold water, slowly heat the water and what happens? The frog dies. It does not jump out. It gets so used to the gradual increase in heat (cost factor) that it does not realize it is heading for certain death. Do not make the same mistake!

South Africa's political heritage: Nelson Mandela epitomized reconciliation—that is simply another word for integration. He had tea with Betsie Verwoerd, the wife of Hendrik Verwoerd, branded as the mastermind behind the apartheid philosophy. Nelson Mandela was driven by positive aspirations. Of course, one would be able to find moments where he did not apply the principle fully, but he constantly defaulted to the integration of positive aspirations.

My father has had the privilege of associating with Nelson Mandela on more than one occasion. In one instance, the members of the press who were present asked Mandela to pose for a picture with former Robben Island inmates. My father moved away from the scene, only to be called back assertively by Nelson Mandela to join him in the picture. This is how a positive aspiration leader acts. He or she always defaults back to integrating with other stakeholders.

General Constand Viljoen, who represented a large percentage of Afrikaners and probably had the power at one stage to boycott or hijack the entire South African miracle, decided to integrate. As a leader, he aspired towards a peaceful transition. So much so that many Afrikaners turned against him when he decided to follow the direction of entering the election process and structures.

His desire was to integrate with all stakeholders, but this was not possible in such a highly volatile and challenging environment. There was a cost of not being able to integrate with all Afrikaners. Some parties boycotted the election process. There were the odd bombs planted by extremists. Ultimately, a few years down the line, Constand Viljoen's political power base declined considerably. He eventually retired from politics.

Did he pay the ultimate price (cost) for not integrating sufficiently with the aspirations of his followers or did he pay the price (cost) of a calculated adjusting strategy? I think it is the latter. As a leader, he accomplished his aspiration of a peaceful and miraculous transition, even though he had to adjust in the process—TiLi!

Lessons learned

If you 'Edo' the profitable movement way, you will move with more confidence towards a 'great leadership' destiny! This means you will make sure that relationships with all other stakeholders are moving profitably in the process. You will continually strive to balance what you want with what your stakeholders want.

- Life is all about movement.
- Leaders are in the business of movement.
- All movement is governed by the integration of motivation, direction and structure.
- We cannot move profitably in isolation.
- Profitable movement is the integration of positive aspirations, integration of directions and the integration of structures of all important stakeholders and compensating/adjusting/adapting when integration does not take place.

CHAPTER FOUR

RESISTANCE TO MOVEMENT

"Mature individuals intuitively understand that resistance to movement is not only possible; it is a process and fact of life"

The Law of Resistance

Let us go back to my 'walking' example, which I use in front of groups to illustrate the Law of Movement. I mention to the group that if only life was as easy as following the Law of Movement or Profitable Movement it would be great. But, there is this other universal law that once again proves life to be simple but contributes towards life being incredibly difficult. It is called the Law of Resistance, which is: All movement, change or growth in life is accompanied by resistance.

No movement, change or growth in life occurs without some form of resistance. What about the simple act of walking in front of the group—is there resistance? Yes, there is. Air pushes against me, gravity pulls me down, and there is friction between my feet and the surface. The resistance is not strong enough to stop my movement, but it is there nevertheless.

Great leaders intuitively grasp the nature of the Law of Resistance to Movement, and understand that resistance to movement is not only possible; it is a process and fact of life—TiLi!

The nature of this life is one of resistance to change on the one hand, and unlimited support for change on the other.

We should not fight the Law of Resistance. The law is our friend. Our actual opposition may or may not be our friend. In other words, the cancer that threatens your life may not be your 'friend' at that moment but the experience (resistance), if you survive, is what sharpens your abilities and wisdom. From a business context, the competition in the marketplace is not necessarily our 'friend', but it does sharpen our abilities and keep us on our toes.

All parents will appreciate the struggle of teaching children the dangers of life. Children often rebel against obstacles that their parents see, but which may be hidden from them (the children) at that stage of their maturity. Ironically, many of us are still childish in the sense that we resent everything that stands in our way. So much of the unhappiness in the world occurs as a result of an immature attitude towards resistance to movement.

It is the universal Law of Resistance to Movement/Change that enables us to grow in every area of life. It is impossible to grow without resistance in some form or another. To hate the Law of Resistance is like a body builder who hates his weights in the gym—he wants big muscles, but he hates the weights! The law is actually our friend! Referring back to the simple act of walking, even though there is resistance in the form of friction between the soles of my shoes and the surface, it is that very friction that helps me to walk. In fact, if it wasn't there, I would have slipped all over the place; I would not have been able to move. The same goes for the Law of Gravity—without it I would have floated all over the place and would not have reached my destination. Immature individuals or leaders see the Law of Resistance as the enemy. Great leaders see it as a friend.

What is the role of resistance and opposition?

Resistance and opposition determine our character, skills and confidence. I asked Matthews Phosa in an interview what made him the man he is today, and he answered, "I think it is many things, like your upbringing, but I think how you then relate to the challenges. Our generation faced many difficult challenges. You had to find a way of learning, studying, while at the same time being drawn into struggles … the University of Life! The whole negotiation process in South Africa was a University of Life to me. We learned to understand each other's points of view, where we came from two extremes yet learned to give and take …"

As mentioned, it is simply impossible to grow without resistance. No muscle can be strengthened without resistance or opposition of some kind, referred to as exercise. No seed can grow, no animal can grow, no talent can be developed, and no success can be experienced, except in the context of opposition and opposites.

Sean Summers, former CEO of Pick 'n Pay, comments as follows about the tough times the company went through over the years, "I think that without those tough times you don't develop; you don't build character."

All persons of substance who I have met are where they are and what they are because of so-called tough times. A short while ago, I had a fascinating meeting with Mark Lamberti, former CEO of Massmart. At the end we got up, and on the way out he made a comment about his respect for Brand Pretorius, CEO of McCarthy Limited. He then added that all people of substance have gone through very tough times in their lives! Part of why he respects Brand so much is because of the way in which he conducted himself during the difficult days at McCarthy when the company almost came to an end.

Ivan Clark, former CEO of Grindrod, moved that business from being a struggling 100 million market cap business to a highly profitable 11 billion market cap business. He says, "Anyone with a desire to be successful is going to have failure, but the big thing is to get up again and to go on. That's what happens with entrepreneurs and people who want to get on with life. Even if they get knocked down in the really early stage of their attempts to do well, they get up. It actually inspires them to do better the next time. You don't want to fail all the time because then you're never going to get there, but you tend to learn from it; you take lessons out of it; it increases your desire to achieve."

They test and refine our aspirations

We cannot really measure the level of passion we have for our own aspirations until we meet opposition and resistance of some kind. The power of positive aspirations is fashioned in your mind and heart by the tribulations of life. How many times have you experienced a situation where you expressed your desire (aspiration) to do something and then quickly changed your mind when the realities of the situation confronted you? Once or many times? The following personal examples illustrate the point:

My father remembers as a child admiring the beauty of a high mountain and he decided to walk to the mountain. An hour later, the mountain was exactly the same distance away. What was happening was that he was confronted with resistance and opposition to his plan by the reality that the mountain appeared to be close by but was in fact much, much further away. He then stopped the walking excursion. It was too difficult!

In life, he evaluates his aspirations to reach the 'mountains' and decides how passionately he really wants to reach his objective.

I hold a 2nd Dan black belt in karate. Most of my life I loved the sport, and still do, because of the universal principles associated with it. At one stage in my life, I went on a two-year voluntary mission. During this time I did not practise the sport at all. I came back a more mature individual as a result of pressures and challenges. My context changed with regards to my aspirations in life. But, when I returned, I tried to carry on with my aspiration to excel in karate, but couldn't. Why? The resistance and opposition of time, energy and physical commitment were too much. Other aspirations of career, studies, marriage and voluntary commitments took precedence, and I was willing and motivated to face the necessary resistance and opposition in these areas of my life. Had I faced the resistance and opposition in my karate career, I could have been a 4th or 5th Dan black belt by now.

Our aspirations are continually being tested and refined in the process of overcoming so-called resistance. Obviously, this only happens if we react in a positive manner towards it.

On the subject of experiencing resistance in your life, Ivan Clark says, "Some people get put down too often as well, by their peers or someone they go to for advice. So I always say to people to be careful of the negative people out there. There will be so many that will say that what you want to do can't be done or, look at what went wrong, instead of saying, 'Look we almost got there and if we do it again we are probably going to get there.' You know, 90 per cent of people want to do well, maybe 99 per cent or even 100 per cent, but it's normally an outside influence that knocks them a little bit. My advice is to use your own ability, use your own thoughts, and when people give you advice absorb what is good from it. But, if you feel that advice is knocking you unfairly or incorrectly, then throw that advice away and carry on with your path. I see it happen often that people that are knocked down don't go on and people that are encouraged even in failure succeed."

Living in South Africa and not understanding or believing that resistance and opposition are valuable for personal development is unfortunate. The South African or even African environment is a breeding ground for opposition and resistance, and so great leadership—TiLi! Perhaps someone who leaves the country permanently for an 'easier' life somewhere else does not fully appreciate this concept. One should not judge others, but it is a point worth pondering.

I spent an interesting couple of hours with Marko Saravanja, the founder of Regenesys Business School. His life was one of absolute contrasts and extremes. In his book, *Secrets of Success*, he writes, "Every great success, in business or in your personal life, begins with a dream or a vision. But the road from dream to reality is full of obstacles … accept that obstacles are there to make you stronger."

They allow us to develop integrated aspirations (unity among stakeholders)

Unity may be the most powerful motivational force, depending on the quality of valued standards driving such unity. In the profitable movement process, integrated positive aspirations are listed as the governing element of motivation. Integrated positive aspirations are really a mature form of unity. Most so-called resistance and opposition are an invitation to work out integrated aspirations with other stakeholders.

I recall receiving a phone call from the PA of Roy Andersen, the then CEO of Liberty. She said he would like to see me because, in her words, he was worried about certain issues in something I wrote (may have been an article). My first thoughts were that I was in trouble of some kind as regards the relationship with him. This was when I'd first started associating with top leaders, so it didn't take much to intimidate me. My second thoughts, in context with the principles of great leadership, were that this was a fine opportunity to further build our relationship—integrate aspirations—and that is the way it turned out. I've met and interviewed him several times since. If I did not have the right attitude towards possible resistance or opposition, the situation may not have turned out positively at all.

They refine us

Every positive attribute of humankind needs to be developed and refined. Should all things always happen without any opposition and resistance of any kind, we would find that our ability to grow would evaporate.

A practical example of this principle can be found in the many instances of a child growing up in a rich and spoilt environment where every whim is catered for. So often such an upbringing has disastrous results for the character of the child. The child was denied resistance to his or her desires and whims in life and thus could not develop positive character traits. To that child, life does not consist of laws and consequences, but of self-indulgent desires without accountability.

Nolo Letele, the CEO of Multichoice, had the blessing of qualifying as an engineer overseas. But, like most leaders worth their salt, he experienced hardships that shaped his character. He grew up without a father, who passed away before he was a year old and when his mother was only 29. Understandably, she had a nervous breakdown at the time, but she recovered from it. She got up again and leaned on her success, which was that of being one of the few graduate woman teachers of her time. So, in Letele's words, "She just ran …" two sons and all. In fact, she ran so fast that they never stayed in one place for longer than two years. Letele sees his childhood days as an experience that assisted him in becoming very adaptable and acquiring excellent people skills. In other words, it refined his character.

Is Nelson Mandela not a perfect example of this principle? He sacrificed freedom in exchange for a truly challenging 27 years in jail. His entire life consisted of resistance and opposition. What did this do for him? Did it break him? No, it made him—refined him!

They enable us to build effective structures in support of our aspirations

It is only by experience (learning and confronting) that we develop the skills necessary to mobilize, optimize, economize and integrate effective structures in support of our aspirations.

An inventor of a great idea came to us for guidance on how to market his product. He had no idea what kind of structural support he needed to market it. He had no idea what resources, production, marketing, capital, systems and facilities he would need to do the job. His visit to us was an example of resistance and opposition to movement because we discussed many so-called problems he would face before getting to market his invention. But, without such resistance, he could not grow and develop his ability to do the job.

It really is impossible to grow without resistance and opposition—TiLi!

Whether one loves or hates Jacob Zuma, one cannot help but have some admiration for him. The man experienced extreme resistance in the run up to the ANC elections. He moved forward despite current and pending court cases, constant investigations into his personal affairs, and media reporting negatively about him, including the publication of nasty cartoon drawings. As I write today, media reports indicate that Zuma is once again being charged for fraud and racketeering, and will appear in court in August 2008. I don't know if he will be found guilty in the future. But, I admire the way he overcomes resistance and opposition. If he had his day in court and the verdict was 'not guilty' and his motives remained pure, he would be a good option for leadership of our country, as he will overcome all odds and resistance. Whether he is as good at creating movement or profitable movement, I don't know exactly, but he can withstand resistance! Usually a leader who can create unity is also skilled at creating movement.

Applying the Law of Resistance to Movement

Resistance to movement is part of each moment of existence. The universe cannot exist without opposition in all things. Physics recognizes this principle with the law that states that all actions have equal and opposite reactions. This truth leads to the following assumptions in the life of a great leader: Expect resistance and opposition as a natural element of movement.

Focus on building trust in processes that empower you to address resistance—become a skilled confronter for example.

No decision will guarantee specific movement. Opposition *will* occur, thus your processes *must* include handling opposition. For this reason you should always include possible resistance factors in your planning. Absolute trust in universal processes is the only power that can rule and overcome all resistance.

When we try to evaluate any form of movement without including possible opposition in the evaluation process, we will increase the risk of ending up in troubled waters—TiLi!

Lessons learned

My parents had a row of tall, rather unattractive blue-gum trees outside their previous home. These trees were able to easily withstand the strong gusts of wind they regularly experienced on top of the small hill where they grew. The trees are a strong reminder of the resilience that is developed by trees (and people!) when they learn to face the winds of life, or confront life's resistance and oppositions.

People who live in an environment with increased resistance and opposition are ironically more privileged and fortunate than those who don't. This is the very reason that a South African environment should produce more great leaders than most other environments. We all admire the Nelson Mandelas of life, but we tend to forget why they are people of substance. It is because they have faced incredible resistance and challenges in their lives and overcome them. Most people understand this conceptually, but they would prefer to find another way of becoming great leaders—an easier route! The best route of all is to understand the Law of Resistance and to turn it into a friend rather than an enemy—TiLi!

The Law of Resistance: All movement, change or growth in life is accompanied by resistance.

Role of resistance and opposition:

- They determine our character, skills and confidence.
- They test and refine our aspirations.
- They allow us to develop integrated aspirations.
- They refine us.
- They enable us to build effective structures in support of our aspirations.
- It is impossible to grow without resistance and opposition.

CHAPTER FIVE

ATTITUDE MANAGEMENT

"People want to follow someone that is positive"— Heyneke Meyer (rugby coach)

Attitudinal modes

Energy! Energy! Energy! This has to be the most effective way of describing Stephen Saad from Aspen. He only sleeps four hours a night, but one gets the impression he could make do with even fewer. He is the founder of Aspen, which today boasts a market capitalization of many billions. They recently acquired a company in South America for about R1 billion. His advice to owners of smaller businesses on how to become successful is to have a plan and a goal, control expenses and stay positive—in other words, manage your attitude. By the way, if I shuffled his formula around a bit you will notice that he quoted the Law of Movement without knowing it—stay positive = motivation; have a plan, a goal = direction; control expenses = structure.

Heyneke Meyer, the brilliant rugby coach who led the Blue Bulls team to a spectacular Super 14 final says about attitude, "As the leader you can't afford to be down. Over the last two years, I have realized that people want to follow someone that is positive, with a vision and that makes plans, even if it goes bad … If you, as the leader, go to them to complain, you push them away and they don't want to follow you. I am positive and it can be tough, but I see it as part of character building."

In approximately 1995, Thoko Mokgosi went for a job interview at Telkom. The post would require her to work with mostly white Afrikaans-speaking males who were more technically skilled than she was. Imagine this situation in 1995, not now in 2007! Add the fact that when she went for the interview she was eight months pregnant. I had the fortunate opportunity of having an interesting discussion with the man who employed her. Of course he encountered some resistance among his colleagues for selecting her. Mokgosi believes, and she is also correct, that she was employed because they were not looking for an engineer, but a business person—a marketer who could help grow the business. But, in speaking to her employer, he said her "demeanour and attitude to life just stood out above all the other candidates." So, here is someone who seemed to have everything going against her in the corporate landscape at the time—a young black woman, technically inferior (wasn't an engineer), and eight months pregnant, yet the situation turned her way. It happened because of her attitude to life. One's attitude and demeanour makes it easier for others to open doors to opportunities. Today, she is the CEO of HP South Africa and Businesswoman of the Year 2007. Mokgosi believes in opening up doors for other people, who in turn will hopefully do the same for others!

Managing your own attitude as well as those you lead is a critical success factor in moving towards becoming a greater leader. But, this skill is very seldom, if ever, taught to leaders during academic studies or anywhere else for that matter, and I include MBA courses in this assessment.

I believe the area that society lacks most in developing or fast-tracking leaders is that of teaching leaders how to manage or move people's attitudes, which is critical to moving people effectively!

In essence, leaders have to move two things—attitudes and/or situations. As Louisa Mojela from Wiphold explains, "Leaders are responsible for moving the bottom line of the company; they are responsible for moving the attitudes of their subordinates and colleagues; they have to move the outward opinions of how the company is viewed outside by either competitors or the market generally. They even have to move the external factors that the company is subjected to."

Often, if the leader is able to move someone's attitude towards a given situation from negative to positive, and that person then looks back at the same situation, he or she may suddenly perceive the situation as acceptable. In other words, the attitude was the problem, not the situation; the person's view of the situation was clouded by negative perceptions and unresolved concerns—some of them real and some perceived. After changing the attitude, which happens by addressing negative perceptions and concerns, the person then shifts into a position from where the situation can be seen clearly. If the situation is still a problem, then it is time to do something about it—move it; change it; improve it.

The South African situation of serious crime is an example. The attitude of a citizen could be negative to the point that he or she wants to leave the country. Theoretically, one could change or move the attitude to where the same individual sees the country as a land of opportunity. Looking back at the crime situation with more clarity will reveal that it is still a problem that must be moved or changed. Now one can start addressing the issue. There is, however, a major difference between a person with a negative attitude and a person with a positive attitude confronting a situation in order to create forward movement.

Great leaders instinctively understand the universal Law of Attitudinal Modes, which is: All human beings perceive all life situations through attitudinal modes.

In other words, every situation you find yourself in has an attitudinal mode between you and the situation. Any situation where people are involved cannot exist without an attitudinal mode present. It is like a window through which you view the situation. If the window is dirty and muddy, your perception of the situation or person on the other side will be unclear, out of context and most likely unrealistic. If the window is clean, you will have a clear and more realistic view of the situation or person.

Leaders have to discern their own mode and that of the person and/or group that they lead. Only then will they be empowered to guide the person or group into the most productive mode, where positive things really happen; where energy exists.

All people experience the various attitudinal modes several times during a given day and even situation. However, people differ dramatically from each other in the way they respond to these modes. We find that a person like Nelson Mandela is driven predominantly by the ideal mode, while a person with very low self-esteem may be driven by the least ideal mode. You will recognize the validity of attitudinal modes as I describe them further.

The attitudinal modes are as follows:

- Negative expectation attitudinal mode
- Positive expectation attitudinal mode
- Negative aspiration attitudinal mode
- Positive aspiration attitudinal mode
- Flux mode

To understand people better, it helps significantly to understand the attitudinal modes and how these impact on people's motivation and perceptions. The attitudinal modes model may appear to many as an over-simplification, but experience gained from thousands of interviewing, counselling, coaching and training sessions proves this approach to be very effective.

Each of the attitudinal modes has distinct attributes. You need to learn to recognize them for what they are. They are key elements in helping you to understand people, how to motivate them and how to eventually move organizations profitably.

Negative expectation attitudinal mode

Negative expectations are an attitudinal mode that everyone is familiar with. It is when you expect something negative to happen before the situation has even occurred. You may need to replace your driver's licence but postpone it to the last possible minute because of a negative expectation that you may have to wait in a queue all day. You have this expectation because of experiences others have shared with you. The truth is that this expectation is merely a perception and not reality. Many have gone there and managed to be back at the office in two hours.

A negative expectation, if entertained too long, will often result in actions that are rather radical or negative, like delaying the renewal of your driver's licence until it is three months overdue. You may have negative expectations about crime in South Africa, or the education system, or whatever. Such perceptions and feelings will fester if not addressed and eventually you will see South Africa through one window—a dirty one. What will you do? You may just pack up and leave.

Or, you may have negative expectations about your teenage son and, if you don't address them, the negative expectations will grow and grow until they dominate. The window through which you view your son will become so dirty that you will not see him for what he is. The same principle applies in relationships with spouses and with staff members. Some people have negative expectations about different races, genders or cultural groups.

Negative expectation mode can include having negative perceptions only about a past situation, probably because you expected negatives beforehand.

In this mode, people feel anxiety at different levels, ranging from everyday concerns—taking a day to renew their licence—to panic attacks. So-called negative people are often in this mode and their lives are inundated with threats, fears and negative expectations. More often than not they expect a negative outcome rather than a positive one. The world of negative expectations is sheer hell for some people.

But, negative expectations are not only being negative. Many genuine concerns may fall into this category. Even so-called positive people often have negative expectations when they have unresolved concerns. One must not simply reject this mode as unreasonable and unacceptable.

For example, it is not unreasonable to expect that the renewing of one's driver's licence may take all day. After all, more people have negative and time-consuming experiences doing it than those who don't. Negative expectation mode is critical in the evaluation process, in that it warns you of things that can possibly go wrong, allowing you to put contingency plans in place.

What mode do many South Africans slip into when the president of the country, or a representative, mentions AIDS? If your answer is negative expectation mode, you are probably correct. South Africans expect some negative, unrealistic or even ridiculous comments. In fact, Thabo Mbeki and his government probably know, or believe they know, how negative the citizens and media of South Africa are about them and their approach to AIDS. So, when a government representative enters a situation where this issue will be addressed at a news conference, in what mode might the government representative be? If your answer is negative expectation mode, you are probably correct again. Now place the two parties that are in negative expectation mode in the same room and what happens? It can be a recipe for disaster if the other attitudinal modes are ignored. How can they communicate positively when both of the parties are looking at each other through dirty windows?

When George W. Bush tried to move nations to support him in launching attacks on Iraq, what mode did many people worldwide slip into? If you remember, it was also mostly negative expectation mode. Unresolved concerns create possible negative expectations, so a negative expectation of many people was that Bush had a hidden agenda about Iraq's oil reserves, especially because of his oil background. Another negative expectation may have been that a war would have had negative economic repercussions worldwide. Are, or were, these negative expectations true? It does not really matter. Perceptions are mostly treated as reality. To the demonstrators worldwide, who marched with posters with slogans condemning George W. Bush for wanting to attack Iraq because of oil, the negative expectations became real.

As mentioned in the introduction, Thabo Mbeki does not seem to be that skilled at managing attitudes, while Zuma seems to be better at it. This means that, if current needs require a unifier, Zuma would be the chosen one, supposing the need to unite was the only or most important criterion of course.

Several serious dangers may flow from the negative expectation mode, especially if you get stuck in it. Often such feelings become self-fulfilling prophecies because you expect them to happen. For example, a cabinet minister expects that a media briefing or a discussion on AIDS with a heavyweight radio talk show host will turn out to be negative. Perhaps the talk show host expects the same? So what happens? The discussion or responses become extremely defensive and even irrational. Participants jump to conclusions, and in the end it turns out to be a debacle.

I received a call from a certain charity organization. The representative asked, "Is this the place that sells glue ...?"

Before I could answer, the individual continued, "Because I am calling from a charity organization and we are making some items that need lots of glue. If you do not sell glue, then would you mind giving a small donation?"

I only managed to answer the first question: "No, we are not the people who sell glue."

The man then promptly hung up. He didn't even wait for a response to the second request for a donation. In what mode was he most likely when he called? Probably negative expectation mode. He expected a negative response to a request for a donation and it became real to him. Generally, sales people should watch out for negative expectations that they themselves breathe life into.

Interestingly enough, negative expectations attract other negative expectations, which is probably why negative people often flock together.

Negative expectations are 'box' feelings. They demand a total authority that they do not have (fear is a good example). In other words, negative feelings tend to shout for attention. They want the world to believe that they will happen and that nothing can stop them from happening. They are box feelings because they have a tendency to feed upon themselves. Their mission in life is to promote their own cause. They are real and they are powerful primarily because we empower them.

There are several signs that may surface when someone is stuck in negative expectation mode. Some of them are negativity in general—all-inclusive negative statements, such as: "Head office is always slow!"; "That guy never has something good to say"; "Government will never get this AIDS thing right"; "The media are always unreasonable"; "I will never be able to accomplish the objectives"; "What you are asking me is definitely impossible to do"; and "No one ever understands me." Other indications are a lack of energy; lack of passion; lack of commitment or ownership; and a lack of innovation.

Negative expectations are a receiving mode, not a commitment mode. In other words, as a leader you have to allow them to be mentioned or identified—receive them. But, do not allow them to take on a life of their own.

Heyneke Meyer's advice or caution is relevant here: "Also remember that if the troops stop bringing problems to you, know you are in trouble."

Your followers, whoever they may be, must feel that they can raise possible or perceived negatives and constraints in your presence. But, what matters is how they raise them! When they treat them as reality, as facts, without reviewing other possible positives that may be as viable as the negatives, then you as the leader must become the balancing factor, or allow someone in the team to take on that role.

Positive expectation attitudinal mode

Positive expectations are mainly conceptual feelings that have a positive or 'nice' connotation. Where one person may expect negative outcomes from a situation, another person may, for whatever reasons, expect positive outcomes from the same situation. Negative expectations are as possible as positive expectations, the latter stimulating hope and feelings that may or may not come to fruition—"Perhaps today the media contingent will go easy on me when I communicate to them about AIDS" or "I am sure Saddam Hussein is not that dangerous and evil." Positive expectations feel good, although they may not be well considered at the time.

Positive expectations are the groping of the mind for positive things. They give the impression of being the opposite of negative expectations. This mode is also a receiving mode, not a commitment mode. In other words, the leader should also allow for positive expectations to be raised in any given situation. Great ideas are often born in positive expectation mode.

I almost want to suggest that it is this mode that keeps us sane, or that at least helps us balance out situations. What happens in reality is that you have a negative expectation one moment, almost immediately followed by a positive expectation.

For example, you may think, "I don't want to renew my driver's licence as it will take all day."

The very next moment you have a thought like, "Perhaps it won't take all day—John told me the other day it took two hours for his to be done." Neither of these thoughts or expectations are or will necessarily come true, but they balance the evaluation process out and make it easier to act or decide. When you actually get to the licence renewal building and it ends up taking a day, there is nothing you can do about it other than start to once again manage your attitude—"This is going to be an awful day" or "Perhaps I will get to know some interesting people in this long queue." By the way, this is exactly what happened to me when I spent a morning renewing my card, three months after the expiry date I might add. I met some interesting and great people! When I eventually got to the counter and discovered that my credit card wasn't good enough for them, my new friend gave me a blank cheque and trusted I would pay him back via the internet. In some situations, the only thing you have control over is your attitude. Be aware of the negative expectations, but exchange them for positive expectations and then move to positive aspiration mode—to be discussed later.

Another example is your boss calling you into her office and you start fluctuating between negative expectation mode and positive expectation mode. The first thought may be "What have I done wrong?" followed by another thought of "Perhaps she has some exciting news for me." In truth, if you walked to her office and allowed your attitude to only consider possible negative expectations you would enter with a very 'dirty window' between you and would not see any of her actions or her message clearly and realistically. First of all, you may be very surprised when she shares some exciting news and perhaps even take a minute to believe her. Or, if she does share bad news, you will absorb it much harder as you are in the wrong mode. You would eventually have to get yourself out of the negative expectation mode in order to move along to solutions and positive actions.

If a staff member storms into your office and starts sharing only negative expectations about another colleague or situation, you should see warning signs all over the place. The chance that many of those negative expectations are not real but perceived is almost 100 per cent. Hardly any situation consists of negative expectations only. A mature staff member will share not only negative expectations, but also balance the report with positive expectations. You see, even if your plane crashed in a desert, your situation would not be negative expectations only. In fact, what would keep you sane in such a situation would be combating or balancing all the negative expectations with positive expectations, so that you do not get stuck in negative expectation mode. Some of those in the group with you will raise negative expectations only, like "We will never be found here" or "What will we eat" or "We will run out of water." As a leader, you would either become the balancing factor by bombarding the team with positive expectations, without ignoring the negative expectations or you will allow those team members who raise positive expectations to have the floor as well. You may say things like "I am sure we will be found" or 'If we put our heads together, we will come up with ways of rationing our food effectively and finding food" or "There must be a way of accessing water." Negative expectations often shout louder than positive expectations though, which means in a crisis situation like this the chance of the entire team getting stuck in negative expectation mode is greater than not. In this situation, the leader would have his or her work cut out, because what the leader wants to accomplish is to get the team into positive aspiration mode where everyone is united around positive desires of staying alive and getting back home. Then the leader would want the team to start putting in place believable and clear directions and actions, followed by structures, in order to move the situation forward successfully. But, the greatest enemy and friend in the situation could be negative expectation mode—greatest enemy because people may get stuck in it and voluntarily die because they allow the negative expectations to dominate and so become real; greatest friend because it will highlight the actual challenges and obstacles that need to be addressed and combated via directions and structures in order to survive and get out of there alive.

Positive expectation mode could also be the greatest enemy or greatest friend in this instance—greatest enemy because positive expectations with no substance and plans will eventually be exposed and push the attitude back to negative expectation mode; greatest friend because in this mode good ideas may flow through discussion of possible solutions.

An organization that is under 'attack' during a hostile takeover, like the Harmony/Gold Fields situation several years ago, will find it challenging to manage the attitude of staff and therefore the organization. The leaders will have to continually process negative expectations by taking note of them, balancing them with positive expectations and then focusing on the positive aspirations, directions and relevant structures that move them towards their aspirations, while addressing the real negative expectations.

Because Harmony was perceived to have failed at the bid, the chances were always there that they could collectively, not necessarily individually, sink into negative expectation mode. The opposite was possible with Gold Fields. Looking at both companies today—beginning 2008—it seems like Gold Fields as a company is in positive aspiration mode and Harmony is in negative expectation mode. Graham Briggs, the newly appointed CEO of Harmony, will have a tough job managing the attitude of the entire company back to positive aspiration mode. Figuratively speaking, they are in the desert.

Signs of being stuck in positive expectation mode may be:

- 'Nice guy' syndrome
- Scared to confront
- Avoiding any negative statements
- Just going with the flow
- At best conscientious
- Passion not necessarily present
- May end up following other people's aspirations rather than own
- May be prone to manipulation

Negative aspiration attitudinal mode

Negative aspirations are the mode you slip into when, for whatever reason, you focus your desires on achieving negative rewards, or implementing negative strategies to achieve certain rewards. You know what you want and go for it no matter what it takes, even if it means taking Nelson Mandela to court or hijacking an aeroplane and deliberately flying it into a building.

The interpretation of what constitutes negative rewards is subjective and depends on your valued standards of behaviour. In terms of great leadership principles, negative rewards would be those that are based on self-indulgent and selfish wishes or desires. Often people who are driven by negative aspirations are considered to be successful by others because of their outward symbols of success they represent, such as position, income, fame and power. In a universal standard context, they are not necessarily successful and often leave behind a legacy of hurt and damage.

Negative aspirations are committed negative desires, not just speculations such as negative and positive expectations. They are powerful motivating forces and are the drive and energy behind many people. Their actions often have negative implications for others, but they are powerful forces nevertheless. Negative politics within the corporate environment is a good example.

An extreme example would be a murderer who is committed to whatever passion drives him, like a terrorist. He does not doubt his purpose and may be very successful within the context of achieving his goal. Hitler was a good example of a negative aspiration person. At a certain stage of his life, he used any means possible to accomplish his aspirations/desires.

A person driven by the commitment to negative aspirations will most likely have a more powerful impact than those with positive expectations only, because a focused desire/aspiration is a powerful motivating force. Perhaps the comment "Nice guys don't win" supports this statement. If the nice guy only has positive expectations without positive aspirations to back him up, he will probably lose.

People with negative aspirations tend to draw upon other people with negative aspirations to realize their desires, and tend to be manipulative of other people. They often rationalize with excuses, such as, "I had no choice in the matter, so I clobbered him."

In short, negative aspiration leaders will apply the movement model and not the profitable movement model. Their own motivations (aspirations), directions and structures are paramount while the motivations, directions and structures of others around them are secondary. Robert Mugabe seems like a great example in this instance. One senses a selfish leader who knows what he wants and he goes for it no matter what. Collectively, the citizens of Zimbabwe seem like good-natured, wonderful people—positive expectation type individuals. A negative aspiration person will always dominate a positive expectation person, which is the case in the beautiful country of Zimbabwe.

Signs of being stuck in negative aspiration mode may be:

- Energy
- Passion
- Innovation
- Deceit
- Commitment and ownership
- Aggression
- Confrontation coupled with negative conflict
- Selfishness
- Enemies
- Judgment and action based on negative expectation input only
- Negative politicking
- Success in terms of self-indulgent symbols
- Negative legacy

Negative aspirations are a commitment (doing) mode.

Positive aspiration attitudinal mode

Positive aspirations are what great leadership is all about. Leaders in positive aspiration mode know what they want—positive outcomes driven by positive valued standards—and they use positive, integrative methods to get there. They use the movement model in an integrative manner. Positive aspirations are the essence of universal motivation and they are responsible for all positive happenings in life. People who are driven by other modes may generate positive things but it is normally in spite of their attitudes and often they get credit for other people's positivity.

Positive aspirations are the result of a disciplined thought process—when an individual consciously tries to establish what his or her aspirations are in life, or in a situation. They are committed desires based on a positive value system or positive standards of behaviour. They have a clear out-of-the-box mentality and identify with all other positive universal standards and attributes. They evoke innovation and initiative and stimulate the best in us and in others.

People with positive aspirations embrace negative expectations and do not fear or reject them. They do not see negative expectations as the enemy but as a significant part of their own creation. They are strong because they are the masters of negative expectations. They don't mind giving negative expectations a hearing. They understand that getting negative expectations out in the open allows for forward movement to positive expectation mode, and then ultimately positive aspiration mode. It is a form of faith and rejection of doubt.

Positive aspirations are not necessarily the same as a positive attitude, although they are strongly related. A person may grow up with a positive attitude and not necessarily understand its dynamics. Positive people often avoid negative expectations.

Signs of positive aspiration mode may be:

- Energy
- Passion
- Innovation
- Commitment and ownership
- High value-system
- Openness
- Assertiveness, not aggression
- No fear of confrontation—can do so with limited or no conflict
- Positivity
- Being proactive
- Boldness

- Emotional and mental maturity

It is simple to gauge when someone is in positive aspiration mode. Recently, I needed some objective business advice from a seasoned leader I could trust. I decided to call John Barry, the founder of Adcorp and author of *Leading from the Front.* I think I called him mid-afternoon. His response was: "What are you doing later this afternoon?" He was just so willing to sit with me and did in fact listen and confidently counsel me for more than two hours, into the early evening. This is the attitude and approach of a positive aspiration person. They are always lifting and building others. I know that John coaches several business leaders and has made a difference in their lives.

Positive aspirations are, in reality, what we would term confidence. Often, when we regard another person as being confident, that person is in fact committed to positive aspirations. They are clearly on their way somewhere! Ultimately, the only kinds of confidence that will last are positive aspirations that are based on legitimate universal laws and processes.

Positive aspirations are the most powerful human motivation. Human beings are driven by many kinds of motivation, including drives such as fear. From a psychological point of view, human motivation may appear to be a very complicated issue. But, a leadership perspective is mostly different from that of the average psychologist.

Generating positive aspirations should always be your major objective if you want to be a great leader. Positive aspirations are the source of all profitable movement and without them nothing positive will happen.

From your perspective as a leader, you also need all stakeholders to default to positive aspirations for the good of everybody concerned. Remember, your mission is to generate positive movement and to do so you must generate positive aspirations.

A CEO that we coached explained that he was sitting in the cafeteria following a difficult acquisition and then a cost-cutting period. Several letters of retrenchment had just gone out, as well as a letter to the rest of the staff. The CEO could feel that the mood in the cafeteria was not good. He could feel that the collective mode was not that of positive aspiration.

This awareness, talk in the hallways, as well as other feedback structures, helped him to realize that there were some negative expectations about a certain word in the retrenchment letter. He realized instinctively that the current environment stimulated negative expectations and so the negative expectation mode. He called a meeting of all staff and addressed the issue. He could identify, predominantly by feeling it, that the mode was wrong, and then acted on it.

Flux mode

Flux mode is that necessary state of mind that we continually experience while we are between modes and in the process of assimilation or evaluation. In practice, most of us are continually in flux mode as we fluctuate between modes, like my examples earlier where a positive expectation thought follows on a negative expectation thought.

Flux mode is a necessary element of the universal process of generating decisions and commitment. This is the mode where we are open to persuasion and have not yet settled into a commitment mode (negative or positive aspiration mode).

People who are in flux mode are in a teachable mode. But, when the flux mode becomes a bad habit, we call it the flux mode syndrome. It is when an individual can't make a decision, over-evaluates, and battles to cross over to the 'do' part of the universal 'Edo' principle. It is now a 'sickness' of the mind. It is an international disease of vast proportions.

Signs of those suffering from the flux mode syndrome may be:

- Inability to make decisions
- Uncertainty
- Lack of confidence
- Cynicism

- Lack of ability to do the job
- Lack of energy
- Lying and fabrications
- Lack of fun and joy
- Lack of compassion
- Anxiety
- Despondency
- Fatigue

Lessons learned

Today, as I write this paragraph, it is 2 January 2008. While walking with my wife this morning, I mentioned to her that people generally are more energetic and even friendlier than usual at this time of year. I described my theory to her that many people are in fact in positive aspiration mode because they have reviewed their year ahead and even set some goals or defined their aspirations. This is why they are more relaxed and in better moods. But, what will happen in the next few weeks? They all start going to work, travelling in the traffic, encountering challenges (Law of Resistance), and therefore come into contact with negative expectations. In many cases, they will allow the negative expectations to drag them down from positive aspiration mode to the negative expectation mode. So, people will once again become more impatient, aggressive and unfriendly. This is how it works and we have to learn to manage our own attitudes.

To summarize further, at the one extreme we have a person who is in negative expectation mode most of the time. He or she may very well eventually become a candidate for suicide. At the other extreme, we have a person who is mostly in a positive aspiration flux mode. In other words, such a person has developed extensive skills in generating positive aspirations as a way of life—he or she evaluates negative expectations, then positive expectations and then shifts into positive aspiration mode.

These are the great leaders of the world. They are the confident people. They stay in flux mode (evaluation mode) while evaluating, with the intention of settling in positive aspiration mode, before making a decision. Although they give the other modes a hearing, they do not allow people or situations to drag them down and if it happens they get out of there quickly.

Another type of extreme would be the person who is continually in the negative aspiration flux mode. In other words, such a person is intensely self-absorbed and motivated towards self-indulgence as a way of life. These are the truly dangerous leaders of the world. They would do anything and everything to achieve their own selfish goals. They stay in flux mode while evaluating, with the intention of settling in negative aspiration mode before making a decision. They may or may not give the other modes a hearing, but if they do it is primarily for selfish reasons—to accomplish their own aspirations.

When people are in attitudinal modes other than positive aspiration mode, they will tend to perceive things in a skewed manner. For example, if you were attending a meeting while in negative expectation mode, you would perceive feelings expressed by a positive person as arrogant, deceitful, unrealistic, out of touch with reality or threatening. However, if other people in the same meeting were in positive aspiration mode, they would perceive the same situation and comment completely differently because they would be evaluating it through a clean window. If I came and discussed the meeting off line with both individuals, I might think they were in different meetings.

When you have an understanding of the attitudinal modes, you will be better equipped to relate to feelings expressed by others. You will be better at transforming negative attitudes into positive attitudes. No longer is it necessary to refer to someone as negative or positive—"John is negative" or "Ann is positive." In other words, you need not and should not label a person, as is so often done in our society. You can simply refer to their expectations as being negative or positive. In other words—

"John has negative expectations." This means you are able to divorce the individual from his or her expectations and in this way deal with the real issues.

In summary, leaders have to move two things—attitudes and situations. All human beings perceive all life situations through attitudinal modes. The five attitudinal modes are:

- Negative expectation
- Positive expectation
- Negative aspiration
- Positive aspiration
- Flux modes

CHAPTER SIX

CONFRONTATION

"Great leaders learn to confront all issues that stand in the way of successful movement"

Confrontation in general

On the way back from Cape Town we always sleep over in the Karoo on a farm called Sarenja. We love it there! In December 2005, we did the same. During breakfast, another visitor arrived and we started a discussion about how people treat one another in life; how the farming community in general is more hospitable than the folk in large towns or cities. The comment was made that my wife and I probably don't even know our neighbours back home. Unfortunately, this was somewhat true. I resolved there and then to change this. The following is an entry in my journal.

"On the farm, I received an impression that when we were back home we needed to walk over to our neighbours, wish them a happy New Year and give them a little something. Things happened over the weekend and we almost didn't do it (resistance—Chapter Four). But, early last night, we walked over and did it. I am so glad we did! We visited almost too long next door and then behind us. The family behind us is a father, mother, and three sons. What a lovely family! They always seemed like a lovely family—swimming together, braaing together, and so forth. As soon as you meet them, you realize that they are good people. As we chatted to them, we picked up on issues that bothered them, mostly in the past and concerning us, their neighbours—tree messing in their swimming pool and the light of the carport shining into their rooms. They didn't come over and chat to us about it, however. People in general are so scared of confrontation. In this instance, even if our neighbours had come over and met us once, left without mentioning the concerns, and then came back a week later to chat about the irritating light that we used to leave on while out in the evenings, their quality of life would have improved."

With both these concerns we'd actually eventually done something on our own. We'd chopped down a part of the tree, unknowingly leaving our neighbour with a smaller mess to deal with. We put lights up on the walls surrounding our property, after my business partner had a gun put against his head in his own garage, so it wasn't necessary to leave the carport light on when we went out for the evening. But, for how long did our neighbours live with the problems, rationalizing their decisions, when they could have approached us about it? We really would have obliged.

Great leaders learn to confront all issues that stand in the way of successful movement. They also learn how to confront! I will discuss this in more detail later.

Why do most people not confront? There are, of course, many reasons, but I will discuss a few.

Often people don't confront because they confuse confronting with two other words—conflict and contention. Most people don't like contention, which is a good thing. But, they don't know how to confront skilfully without contention, so they decide to ignore, rationalize or procrastinate. How do they rationalize? They say things like "I don't enjoy fighting with people" or "We need to be patient with other people" or "The light shining into our bedrooms is not that bad." People procrastinate often for the same reasons, or they give reasons like "I am too busy" or "I have more important things to do than to go over there." The real truth is that they have not yet developed trust in a confrontation process that leads to success. In other words, they are not confident confronters. Unfortunately, most people are not, and this is why we have unresolved grudges that eventually lead to contention that is irreversible, or even war.

The word conflict does not have to mean quarrel or argument. It should rather mean disagreement or difference, which mostly is a good thing. Alfonso Lopez (see last chapter) emphasized the truth to me that all human beings are unique, different and complex. It is therefore reasonable to expect differences or conflicting ideas, perspectives and views. Imagine what the world would be like if we all agreed.

Many people are so busy trying to be what they perceive to be 'nice' that they forget or neglect to confront. They believe confronting is not consistent with being a 'nice' person. They forget that the greatest leaders and individuals in the history of the world learned to confront those resistance factors that prevented them from moving forward successfully.

There are three types of confronters:

1) ***The non-confronter***. This person simply stays away from confronting. He is scared for many reasons, some mentioned above. He will never become a truly great leader!

2) ***The aggressive confronter***. This is a person who has learned the importance of confronting in order to create successful movement, but because he has never learned how to do it properly, he confronts aggressively and gets away with it. Most people are poor confronters, so this person scares them off and gets what he wants. The aggressive confronter may become successful in life, but will battle to move people successfully. Their attitude towards him will mostly be negative.

3) ***The skilful confronter***. There are unfortunately too few of these individuals walking the earth. If only we had more, then there would be fewer divorces, unsuccessful partnerships and wars.

Adrian Gore said the following about confronting so-called problems: "I have found that, when you have problems, there is a moment in time when you turn and face it, and you sort of accept it emotionally and intellectually, and you take a run at it; that's when you are at your best. When you are running from the problem, not only does it catch you and eat you up but it is also very de-motivational. How you motivate yourself is to attack the problems."

I could not have said it better myself.

How to confront skilfully

To confront must be one of the most valuable skills you can learn in life, and it must be one of the most difficult. There are many models out there and eventually you must adopt one that works for you. One of the Boss of the Year finalists referred to 'courageous talks' with her staff. That resonated with me because it takes courage to confront someone about a sensitive issue.

I have coached many leaders to apply a confronting process that, when done correctly, resulted in confidently handling so-called impossible situations between individuals. In one instance, the relationship between two managers who were critical to the business had deteriorated to the point where one party had already been asked to leave the organization. The HR director asked the MD for one more chance to apply this process that he and his associate had been coached on. The result—six months later they were still working together, and even talking to one another. Was it always smooth sailing thereafter? Of course not! Like a marriage, all important relationships need constant nourishment and attention—some more than others.

The steps in the confronting process are drawn from another universal process that successful leaders use to propel profitable movement forward. My father and I coined the leadership process the 'Destiny Chain', which means, in short, that every 'link' in the 'chain' is critical towards a successful outcome (destiny). Most seasoned leaders apply the Destiny Chain subconsciously because it consists of the Law of Movement and profitable movement principles, 'Edo' factor and the Law of Resistance. (It also correlates with the steps in the next chapter.) When they skip any one of these links, they pay a price. Why do they at times skip a link, or some of the links? Many are not consciously aware of the process, and if you are not aware of any process, you are bound to make mistakes, and of course one cannot fine-tune and even transfer the skill. The confronting process makes use of the same underlying universal concepts of the Destiny Chain to increase the odds of a successful outcome. It works—TiLi.

Before I introduce the steps, please note that I will be using two very simple examples, including my experience with the neighbour, to illustrate the steps more practically. Don't think that the examples involve situations that seem too easy to resolve. I am astounded at how often leaders in high positions—even CEOs—allow the most simple situations to get out of hand because they did not confront them early enough. Too often, senior leaders prefer to ignore confrontation sessions. Yes, even at the highest levels, leaders hope situations between individuals will somehow resolve themselves.

The steps are as follows:

1) Commence with the facts of the situation

Once you become aware of a relationship problem or potential relationship problem, call a meeting with the people concerned, or simply walk over to them informally. At this initial stage, it is usually difficult to define facts, so keep things as simple as possible, for example—"Let us discuss the relationship between the two of you, Sanjay and Hazel" or in the case of a neighbour "Can we please chat about your carport light that is sometimes left on at night?" Ensure that there is no judgment or emotion in your introduction statement. For example, ideally you should avoid introducing the situation as, "Let's discuss the bad relationship between the two of you" or "I would like to chat about the fact that you are so inconsiderate in always leaving your carport light on when you go out for the evening." If you put it this way, you assume your neighbours have been doing it while aware of the effect on you. They will feel as though they are being judged without stating their case and will most likely jump into defensive or attack mode, depending on their personalities.

2) State the perceived negative issues in the relationship

With the situation between Sanjay and Hazel find out the problems and constraints the two people involved are dealing with. Let them list their problems without discussing them, all the time emphasizing that you are talking about 'possible' or 'perceived' negatives. Sanjay may feel that Hazel does not greet him each morning, but this may merely be a perception, so do not allow either person to defend or judge actions, although you may ask for clarification where necessary. Remember that people are scared of confrontation in general and do not know how to handle it. Do not look for solutions at this stage.

In dealing with the neighbour issue, you will simply mention your perception of the negatives with as little emotion as possible—"The light shines into our bedrooms, making it difficult to sleep" and not "You don't even consider the inconvenience of leaving your light on—we cannot sleep!"

3) Consider the other side of the coin and/or state the possible positives

In the case of Sanjay and Hazel, you will lead them towards stating the positive or constructive aspects of their daily dealings with one another. Ask them what works. If they do not process the negative aspects of the relationship by exploring the possible positives, both parties will continue to fixate on the negatives. By discussing the possible positives, you now move a few steps closer to finding out what they are really looking for in the relationship. At this stage, you can begin to look for possible solutions to their problems, but without asking for any form of commitment yet—brainstorm the possibilities.

The situation with the neighbour is a little bit simpler in that you need to consider the situation from the other party's perspective. You will follow your possible negative statement of "The light shines into our bedrooms, making it difficult to sleep" with "I know it is possible that you do not realize this and that you probably have a good reason for doing it, like security."

4) Create and agree on positive 'wants'

Look at creating and then agreeing on positive 'wants' in order to begin creating motivation in the relationship. In the case of Sanjay and Hazel, you could ask them what they are ideally looking for in the relationship. What do they want from it? What would they commit to? Once they have articulated that, ask them why. In this way, you will be drilling down to what they are really seeking from the relationship, while gaining deeper insight into who they are.

With the neighbour situation, you would follow the possible positive statement of "I know it is possible that you do not realize this and that you probably have a good reason for doing it, like security" with "We really want a great relationship with you as our neighbours and we are sure you want the same."

5) Agree on actions

It's now time to agree on actions that will help you to address the challenge and even achieve the listed wants. More specifically, in the case of Sanjay and Hazel, you would list your combined actions. Discuss how you are going to get there. Go back and address the negatives now that you know what the two people want. The clear 'wants' will serve as a motivation to positively address the problem areas. Help them to focus on the positives and commit to them.

As a neighbour, you would follow the stated want of "We really want a great relationship with our neighbours" with "How can we address the carport light issue together?" I am willing to bet that in 90 per cent of such cases the neighbour would have obliged after the first step. They would probably have interrupted you with words to the effect of "Oh my goodness, we didn't know or even think of the possibility that the light may inconvenience you—we apologize." But, for the purposes of the exercise I will continue with the example.

6) Discuss and agree on the necessary resources to ensure the achievement of wants and selected actions

Without the resources, no idea can move forward. In essence, you need to look at the actions and decide what resources you need to allocate towards accomplishing them. If Sanjay and Hazel had to share a computer and it is clear that each need their own, then you would allocate budget for this, or you would purchase another computer and commit to doing it by a certain time.

The neighbour situation may not be that clear cut. Your neighbour may already have committed during step five to not leaving the light on in the future. If not, because the neighbour wants to keep it on for security purposes, then the discussion may revolve around other possible resources needed—like building the wall higher, or putting up other lights.

7) Discuss the possible costs of not doing the actions

This means ensuring that Sanjay and Hazel are aware of the cost of not working towards the solution of the problem (performing the necessary actions), and consequently doing whatever is necessary to get the ship back on course—adjusting. Ask them what course of action would be necessary should these consequences arise, or should they not follow through on the plans. What would be the impact on the company if the current discussion does not solve any of the issues? Talk about negativity and loss of productivity. They must own the possible positive outcome, as well as the possible negative outcome, so let them do most of the talking.

This discussion may not be necessary with your neighbour. However, should a clear plan of how to deal with the situation be on the table, it may be wise to throw in a line like, "Thank you for understanding. I'm so glad that we could discuss this openly because if we didn't come to some solution the situation may have impacted negatively on my son's matric exams. When situations like this are not resolved, they often cause unnecessary bad blood between neighbours."

8) Follow through

With Sanjay and Hazel, you decide when and how you are going to follow through on the decisions taken and the progress that may or may not have been made. Hold them accountable!

As far as the neighbour is concerned you must at least give positive feedback when they action the decisions taken. If they simply don't do what they said they would, you may have to act tougher. However, depending on the standard that you have set on being a good neighbour, you may want to Do-Done the situation again. Always remember that the stronger the relationship between people the more motivated they are to agree on the wants, actions and resources. In other words, do not have this confrontation session with the neighbour and never again make contact. Do-Done the situation and follow through with a lovely baked cake, or invite them for a braai. Trust me—this will go a long way in motivating them to do what they committed to doing. My friend, Colin Hall, former CEO of Wooltru, would say that if the energy in the relationship is high or positive it is much easier to have a 'confrontational' discussion; there will be openness and a strong desire to make it work.

9) Reiterate the wants

Summarize your discussions up to this point. Remind Sanjay and Hazel what it is that they want, and what the company is expecting from them. In other words, ensure that you end off on a positive note.

With your neighbour you would simply state something like, "Look forward to getting to know you guys."

The process may seem long for a simple situation like the one with the neighbour, but let's summarize and you will see exactly how quick it is:

You: Pete, can we please chat about your carport light that is sometimes left on at night [introducing the facts, without perceptions or emotion].

Pete: Sure we can, is there a problem?

You: Well, the light shines into our bedrooms, making it difficult to sleep [stating the perceived negative]. I know it is possible that you do not realize this and that you probably have good reason for doing it, like security [consider the other side of the coin]. But, we really want a great relationship with you, our neighbours, and trust you want the same [create and agree on positive wants], so how can we address the carport light issue together? [agree on actions]

Pete: You guessed it correctly, it is a security issue. But, we really didn't realize that it bothered you. Thanks for bringing it to our attention. When we come home, though, it really is dark, so I need to make another plan then.

You: Well, is there a way I can help? If you need to put up another light I can always assist. I know a little bit about electric work [discuss and agree on the necessary resources].

Pete: No, don't worry. I was planning on putting lights down our driveway soon. I will call on you if I need you.

You: Thank you for understanding. I'm so glad that we could discuss this openly, because if we didn't come to some solution the situation may have impacted negatively on my son's matric exams. When situations like this are not resolved, they often cause unnecessary bad blood between neighbours, don't they? [discuss the possible costs of not doing the actions] We will invite you for a braai some time [follow through]. Look forward to getting to know you better [reiterate the wants].

Although the above process is simple, it is not necessarily easy to apply. Nothing worthwhile comes easily. But, everything worthwhile is simple, once you understand it. It takes discipline and courage, above all—discipline to practise and courage to apply. As you do, however, your trust in the process will improve and so too will your confidence as a skilful confronter.

Lessons learned

The ability to confront resistance factors to productive relationships is a critical skill in people interaction and I believe a core competency for you to move with confidence towards your destiny as a great leader. You must not hesitate to invest time and money in improving your confrontation abilities because the cost of not learning to do so confidently can be enormous—TiLi!

"Great leaders learn to confront all issues that stand in the way of creating successful movement"

There are three types of confronters:
1) the non-confronter
2) the aggressive confronter
3) the skilful confronter

How to confront skilfully:

- Commence with the facts of the situation.
- State or write down (if you are writing) the perceived negative issues in the relationship.
- Consider the other side of the coin and/or state the possible positives.
- Create and agree on positive 'wants'.
- Agree on actions.
- Discuss and agree on the necessary resources.
- Discuss the possible costs of not doing the actions.
- Follow through.
- Reiterate the wants.

CHAPTER SEVEN

GREAT LEADERSHIP IN SOUTH AFRICA

"South Africa is the real experiment"

Introduction

So, there you have it. Chapters Two to Six explained some of the critical universal laws and principles that we have found great leaders apply, mostly subconsciously—'Edo' factor; Law of Movement and profitable movement; Law of Resistance; Law of Attitudinal Modes; and confronting. Somehow, great leaders manage to encapsulate all of these laws and principles into one process to create any kind of movement—in themselves, their relationships (confrontation—Chapter Six), their division, their business, their country, or their sports team. As you apply these laws and principles, they will give you a level of confidence in dealing with people and life situations, as described in Chapter One.

In this chapter, I will summarize the laws, add comments and then throw in one other principle that we have noticed is part and parcel of the make up of great leaders. This is the ability to define situations factually.

1) Defining situations factually

Great leaders have the ability to define all situations factually. In other words, when a situation confronts them, they don't allow emotions to 'hijack' their thinking. This takes incredible maturity! Evaluate for a moment how well you apply this principle. It is not easy! When an emotionally ridden situation or an individual who is in an emotional state approaches you, it is very difficult not to get carried away and react emotionally. For example, when you calmly ask your teenager to wash the dishes and he reacts emotionally, it is very difficult not to react emotionally in return, by shouting at him and chasing him to his room.

How did Herschelle Gibbs react when a section of a crowd reacted emotionally towards our South African cricket team? You may remember that he reacted emotionally by swearing, and he paid a price for it. One of my earlier business mentors, Tom Creamer, used to encourage me as a young manager in a large corporate not to get so emotionally charged when debating issues in management meetings. At that stage, I thought he was wasting his breath, but I have come to understand that he was absolutely correct! However, I am still working on it. Others may find it easier because it comes naturally, but this is not the case for me.

When you react while in an emotional or negative mode, you will usually not be coming from a mature perspective. You will probably not realize your actions are negative and will justify them by saying that you are merely addressing a specific situation that is negative. Occasionally, some good may come out of your negative reaction, but this is not very common.

A leader who continually reacts negatively when confronted with crisis situations may try to compensate by using considerable charm. A parent may, for example, buy the child something to make up for the emotional outburst, or take the child to a movie and think things are now okay. But, it is not an alternative for a mature and positive reaction, which is probably to apologize, or admit you were wrong or that you overreacted. In a business set-up, colleagues and employees may abandon ship, as loyalty and unity are seriously threatened when leaders react negatively.

The ability to define situations factually is a skill that applies in any occupation, whether you are a doctor, attorney, teacher, business manager or salesman. When attorneys are faced with a highly emotional case, their ability to remain rational and define the situation factually will go a long way towards engendering confidence in their client and other stakeholders.

A business manager plans for the following year by first defining the facts of the past year clearly, looking at the facts at his disposal for the year ahead, and then strategizing around that. The greater your skill at gathering facts about any situation, while keeping emotions at bay, the greater your ability to make the right decision! Emotion in the wrong place or at the wrong time jeopardizes your ability to stick to the facts.

2) Confrontation

Chapter Six on confronting explains in more detail my feelings and thoughts on the principle. But, just to add briefly, there are far too many leaders in important positions (parents, managers, etc.) who fear confrontation and as a result postpone or ignore the inevitable! You have to confront any obstacle or constraint to successful movement forward!

Great leaders confront negative expectations (constraints, problems, challenges, obstacles) in a certain way, because they have that instinctive respect for the Law of Resistance. They confront them boldly and openly, and where appropriate they will involve as many participants as possible to identify the constraints. Interestingly, though, they treat negative expectations as possibilities or perceptions during the early stages of the evaluation process. How do they do this? When attendees mention concerns or issues, they do not immediately defend and/or judge what comes out. They respect that perceptions are in most cases a reality to people.

Some leaders go to all the trouble of arranging events such as staff lunches or breakfasts where they informally ask staff how they are doing. They invite them to talk about concerns or even possible constraints (negative expectations) that they are aware of in the company. When a staff member mentions a concern, the leader blasts the person from all angles, defending the situation and judging what was said. What goes on in the minds of the other staff members in attendance? “I’m not going to raise my concerns. My boss is going to blast me in front of all my colleagues." Very soon no concerns are raised and the leader walks away thinking that he or she has done a good job and that staff have no complaints.

Nolo Letele from Multichoice is comfortable enough with himself that he will call in one of his team members and openly and honestly ask, "What am I doing wrong with the team? What can I do better?" He may receive some excellent feedback there and then, or not. But, such an action may build up the confidence of his team members, allowing them to feel that they can comfortably approach their leader in the future about something that they perceive to be 'out of place' in the team.

Not many leaders ask for such blunt feedback! Many would call you in and ask you in an almost clandestine manner your opinion of other team members, making you believe that they trust you more than the others and that they would never do the same behind your back. Watch out for this!

Not that it is necessarily wrong to ask the opinion of one leader about another. But, it should be done with pure motives, sincerely, in an environment where there is a culture of existing respect and openness and where the leader allows for himself or herself to be scrutinized in the same manner as the other team members. If not done in such an environment, the culture becomes one of fear, dirty politics and even hostility.

It is crucial that the leader allows for a brief time period where concerns, issues and worries are listed and noted—allowing people to empty the negatives from their minds. Later on in the process, the listed negatives are addressed when putting certain directions and actions in place.

Please remember that this principle of confronting applies if you want to be a great parent leader as well. Many leaders may apply the skill of confrontation very successfully at work, but when they get home they seem to leave all their leadership skills at the office. Why? Perhaps they don't really see the role of being a father, mother, husband or wife as being that of a leader. It may very well be the most important leadership position you will ever hold! In fact, it is so important that you are never released from it. Your leadership role as CEO, manager or government minister will come and go, but being a mother or father is a lifelong commitment.

3) Recognize possibilities

(*see* Chapter Five)

In other words, don't only see the obstacles ahead but also see the possibilities. Be an optimist. Using my example above, when those in attendance at the breakfast have listed the perceived negatives, great leaders change the attitude in the room by inviting attendees to also evaluate the positives of the given situation. They simply ask for comments on what has gone right or what has been done well or what is good about what happened. In this way, they change the mood in the room to a more optimistic one, and they prepare the minds and hearts for a discussion on positive aspirations.

Great leaders are brilliant at creating an optimistic environment, because they generally are optimistic themselves. I asked Adrian Gore why he was so successful and his answer in part was, "I am an optimist … There is a natural positivity in the way I operate, so there is a huge amount of fuel to keep doing things ... I work at being positive. I have an innate belief that you can make a difference ..."

When you are bombarded by perceived negatives ahead, take note of them, and at the correct moment put contingencies in place, but don't fixate on them. Start seeing the possible positives about the situation as well as the possible opportunities. Don't accept only negative input about any situation or person; insist on exploring the other side of the 'coin'. This is especially important when someone shares one-sided negatives with you about another person. An immature leader would be swept away by the moment and even make a judgment call based on one-sided information. But a great leader will never accept one person's input only, especially if it has a negative tone and can affect another person's reputation or future. My mentor, Tom Creamer, decided to hear my side of a situation that potentially could have had devastating affects on my future. Because of great leadership, he positively affected the course of my career. In the context of this leadership quality, it is therefore not wrong for Mr Mbeki to try to express a positive statement about crime not being out of control, or for the commissioner of police to state, "I want to say now that 2010 will come and pass … just like the Rugby World Cup passed." But such statements are only valid and uplifting when the leaders have managed to clearly acknowledge and show that they are confronting the obstacle of crime in SA effectively.

4) Create profitable movement through unity (integration)

(*see* Chapter Three)

I asked my mentor Tom one day why he was successful. His answer was short: "I get things to move." As mentioned in Chapter Three, for any movement to occur there must be motivation (mutually agreed upon aspirations); direction (plans/strategies on how to accomplish aspirations and address constraints); and structure (resources, systems, etc.). Without a buy-in to aspirations there will be no sustainable motivation and passion, or committed hearts. Without realistic directions, a logical belief that the goal can be achieved will be absent—there will be no buy-in from the logical left brain. Without relevant structures, such as, for example, money, physical movement will not be substantial or even possible.

In an interview with Russell Loubser, the CEO of the JSE, he made the following comment, which basically describes the Law of Movement: "It is vital for an organization to start off by understanding why they are there [motive], because from there you can develop your strategy [direction], and from your strategy you can develop your structure and you can put your people in place."

No wonder the JSE is the *Financial Mail* 2006 news story of the year!

However, very few leaders can effectively ensure the presence of all three of these principles, and among those who can draw together all three, few can continually balance them effectively. More often than not, a leader has a natural inclination towards, or talent for, one of the three. For example, Thabo Mbeki, in my opinion, is very strong directionally, but he is weaker motivationally—the ability to integrate aspirations of all stakeholders. Perhaps this is why there is so much disunity in the alliance, although I wouldn't want to try and integrate such diverse aspirations myself. If he understands that he is more directionally gifted and accepts it, he can compensate by surrounding himself with leaders who are stronger on the motivational front. Nelson Mandela was stronger in the motivational area and he and Thabo Mbeki should have made a formidable team, barring other factors.

I am convinced that the level of unity in a team (integrated aspirations, directions and structures) equals the level of performance. In other words, if there is 50 per cent unity, then the team is performing at 50 per cent of their potential. The more unity, the more energy, Colin Hall would say.

I interviewed Dr Reuel Khoza on the Leadership Platform. I was most impressed with the man! His level of intellect is almost intimidating, and may have been, were it not for his depth of humility. This is a man who essentially started his career as a 'garden boy', herdsman and cleaner of chalets in the Kruger Park. He is now a chairman on several company boards, including Nedbank and Murray & Roberts Cementation, and is the former chairman of Eskom.

During the show, I sketched the following scenario for him, using my regular panel member, Sean Donnelly, as the guinea pig. If Sean were to be made the leader of some organization, and soon after there were regular reports of disunity, back-stabbing, in-fighting and aggression in the boardroom, what would it indicate about him as a leader? Dr Reuel Khoza's answer was, "I think it effectively says he is providing leadership without consultation; leadership without understanding the need to co-habit with other opinion contributors in the organization." He went on to explain that over time he had crystallized a few values which he believes together make for effective leadership. These values create 'server' leadership, which boils down to an attitude of "I am at your service." The server leader lives essentially by the tenets of consultation, persuasion, accommodation and co-habitation. Such a leader effectively shuns coercion and domination. Dr Khoza then referred back to the scenario I sketched for him earlier and said, "I would say that Sean has failed to shun coercion and domination ... A server leader would be compassionate and humane."

Dr Khoza's comments had me thinking after the show about continual reports in the media regarding disunity, back-stabbing, in-fighting and aggression in the boardrooms of sports, political and labour union bodies, such as Cosatu. If the media reports are remotely accurate and we accept Dr Khoza's input on what effective leadership entails, then we actually have leaders in high positions who are leading according to a lower standard. They are failing "to shun coercion and domination". On the one hand, we hold some of these very leaders up as successful; as the best of the best; as examples of successful leadership. But, on the other hand, we forget to look at the fruits of their labours—disunity, back-stabbing, in-fighting and aggression.

Many top leaders don't seem to understand the universal leadership truth: The level of unity in a team equals the level of performance!

5) Do the tough things

(*see* Chapter Three)

When I meet and/or interview top leaders I quickly sense two things about them:

1) I feel comfortable and know that they want to, can and will integrate with my aspirations if at all possible. In fact, I mostly feel comfortable

enough to call them by their first names.

2) If I don't play ball, they can and will act tough. In other words they will 'adjust' the situation. However, many leaders in very senior positions often battle to act tough and confront obstacles to movement, especially when the obstacle ends up being a person.

Last year, I facilitated a Q&A evening between Ingrid Kast, CEO of DAV Professional Placement Services (top company to work for in 2006 survey) and a small audience of about 25 people at the Saxon Hotel. Someone asked her what the toughest thing she ever had to do as a leader was. Her answer was when she had to let her first employee go. Having to act tough, or having to make tough decisions, is part and parcel of being a great leader. You cannot get away from this fact!

In an interview with Tony Leon, former leader of the Democratic Alliance, the official opposition party, I asked him what his leadership model or approach was, and one of his principles was, "Leadership is about making some very tough decisions and sticking with them … the ability to stand up alone if necessary and defend what you believe in."

This principle goes hand in hand with the skill of confronting. You cannot act tough, or in most cases should not act tough, without having confronted the source. In other words, if one of your children came to you and told you that her brother pushed her into the pool, don't act tough by relaying a message that he must now get out of the pool or go to his room. You don't know what happened there! You are being a poor leader by making a judgment call and acting tough based on emotion and not facts.

Exactly the same principle applies if you manage a business and want to make a tough decision that could be riddled with emotion. Imagine a situation where one of your executives wants to transfer a key player in his team because he does not get along with him. What do you do? Do you just give him free reign or do you inquire to what extent he has sat down with that individual for a constructive confrontation session? If the answer is, "Well we have had some chats, but it's just not working" do you leave it there? Do you ask for more details about how your executive structured these chats or what exactly was said during those sessions? As mentioned earlier, my experience is that just because someone is on a senior level it does not mean they can confront effectively. Even individuals at the highest levels may shy away from confrontation. A good leader will realize that the person who is not there cannot defend himself, and it is his job, as the leader, to ensure that facts are reviewed, rather than emotion adhered to, before tough actions are carried out. There will be times when the leader decides to go straight to the source because his or her intuition prompts her to do so, or he or she will go to the source by having both parties present.

6) Evaluate and re-evaluate fanatically

(*see* Chapter Two)

Assess or measure the desired movement towards agreed upon aspirations, directions and structures, then follow up with, and hold accountable, the relevant individuals. A wise man once said, "When performance is measured, performance improves, but when performance is measured and reported, the rate of improvement accelerates."

Even great leaders neglect to evaluate and re-evaluate positive aspirations, directions and structures on a regular basis. They put dynamic plans in place and get projects to move, but then they often get bored and want to start something new. This even happens in families—perhaps the family produced a plan or schedule of who washes dishes when, but one month later the plan is not evaluated and is left to eventually fizzle out. Months later, the family sits down and decides on another plan.

Evaluating and re-evaluating can become somewhat boring and even monotonous, but it is critical. If not done consistently, ownership is not taken and, ultimately, accountability neglected.

The Leadership Platform team together with Theo Garrun (*Star* 'Workplace' editor) visited Mponeng Mine of the AngloGold Ashanti

Group a while ago. Although the group at that stage was not performing well, this specific mine was. One of the strengths of the senior management team was the ability to fanatically evaluate (assess) and re-evaluate. The spirit of accountability spread across the entire mine!

7) Surround yourself with the best

It is amazing how some leaders have the knack of surrounding themselves with the 'right' individuals. Other leaders just get it wrong! What is right for one leader is of course not right for another leader. I just find that the better you know yourself, the more likely it is that you will get this one right. Consciously or subconsciously, you will surround yourself with other leaders who complement your possible weaknesses, shortcomings or those areas that simply don't interest you. Bottom line, have the guts to get to know yourself!

I had an interesting discussion over lunch with John Barry. He mentioned how they used to ascertain what key leadership skills their senior leaders needed in context to the specific business. They would then evaluate each leader on how he or she measured up against that particular skill set, but they knew that no leader could ever be strong in all those skills. So they expected leaders to have the maturity to indicate how they would address their weaker areas. I suppose that in many instances the strategy for addressing weaker areas was to ensure those skills existed within other team members.

Ivan Clark, former CEO of Grindrod, comments that while they had a bit of luck in deciding to go into the shipping market when it was in a slump, it wasn't only luck, because he had people who knew what they were doing, which he says is very important—people who know the business.

Ian Cockerill referred to the following quote: "Behind every successful leader is an exhausted team." He explained that a successful manager is only successful because of what he or she can achieve through others.

In the family context, surround yourself with best friends, experts and, of course, ensure that you hook up with the best partner possible.

8) Become confident in the areas of technical, people and life

(*see* Chapter One)

Become very competent in some technical field that you love; become competent in dealing with people and learn to love them; become competent at engaging life and love it! If you choose to remember one paragraph in this entire book, then let it be this one—TiLi!

When you choose to become competent in a field that you love, the following will probably happen. You will be happier and you will be more successful. In a larger organization, you will be given more responsibilities, which invariably means you will move into management positions and your field of expertise will slowly move towards that of leadership only, which is a technical field in and of itself. Then you will have to somehow become more competent at being a leader—points 1 to 8 above—and you will have to learn to love leadership, as you did your original field of expertise. To be a competent leader who loves the technical field of leadership is synonymous with being competent in dealing with people and loving them, and being competent in engaging life and loving it! So, you will come full circle!

If you choose to become competent in a field that you love, and you work for yourself, you and your business will become more successful. In other words, your business will grow and expand, and invariably you will end up having to manage more people and departments. Yes, once again your field of expertise will move towards that of leadership, and away from your original expertise, which means you must become competent in dealing with people and loving them, and you must become competent at engaging life and loving it!

Russell Loubser had an interesting and effective way of explaining the need to become confident in some technical area. He said that key things he has learned over the years are that your background for the job you are doing is very important. It helps to have a power base of some sorts when you are placed in the leadership position. That power base can assume different identities. It can be because you started the business or own the business, or because your knowledge of the business is recognized as being superior. Without any powerbase, you make it extremely difficult for yourself. You will have to rely on charm and other things that are not substantial. Because of this power base, you are able to step into the position and know what you like and what you don't like. Russell, for example, had used the financial markets for most of his adult working life, which made it easier to know what he wanted to change or not change at the JSE.

As mentioned in Chapter One, I believe Brand Pretorius, the CEO of McCarthy Limited, is one of the best examples of someone who is confident in all three areas. He has been in the motor industry almost his entire working career. He loves motor vehicles and the industry, and he has become very competent at it. He is seen as one of the foremost experts in the country in this industry. The result is, he moved up the ladder and became the MD of Toyota, and eventually the CEO of McCarthy Limited—a company with more than 6,000 staff and a R19 billion turnover. When I interviewed several individuals who have known Brand for many years, and then met and interviewed the man, I immediately realized that he loves people and he is very competent in dealing with them. The skill that he is possibly most competent at in dealing with people is listening—the importance of this skill in being a good leader comes up in almost every interview I do. Brand is one of the few leaders I know who is actually good at it. When I met him personally, I felt important, and I felt like I was at that moment the most important thing in his world. Brand has a passion and energy for life! His mission most certainly revolves around people: lifting them up and helping them become the best they can be.

9) What you are

What you say and do does not matter as much as what you are. This principle dawned on me when I met Alfonzo Lopez. He is from Mexico, but he has been a real globe trotter. He has lived and worked successfully in North, Central and South America, Africa and other places. For the past 18 months, he and his family had been living in Phalaborwa, right next to the Kruger Park. How did they land up there? He gathered his family around him and asked where in the world they wanted to live. They answered Africa, because of a previous positive living experience in Kenya (18 months), and because they love wild animals.

Well, they packed up and left. While on the plane, they thought of living in Namibia, but they were not sure. When they landed at O.R. Tambo International Airport in Johannesburg, they met someone who suggested Phalaborwa, because it is safe and of course close to the Kruger Park, so they decided that was the place to be. They went there in search of a home, which they found, and then they enjoyed a quality of life that they chose. Did they live there forever? No, and does it matter? The question is, why did they do this? Why would a man who already earned $24,000 per month when he was 24 years of age (he is now 48), who wrote a very simple book, which is endorsed by Dr Stephen R. Covey, do this? Well, let me tell you a little more about him.

He heard about what I and my partners do—take leaders on a journey towards becoming great leaders, and decided he wanted to meet us. He set up an appointment for 15:00 on a specific day. Shortly before the scheduled time, I received a call in which he apologized because he would be a couple of minutes late as the taxi still wasn't there to collect him as arranged. It suited me fine. He arrived with an overnight bag in hand. We discussed leadership, life and much more. Everything he said was interesting and impressive! He gave me a copy of his book—*Multiply your Total Capacity in Twenty Minutes*. He was pleasant—courteous, kind, giving and friendly. His actions started to shout louder than his words. After the appointment, he thanked me for the meeting, picked up his bag and said goodbye. I asked him where he intended lodging for the night, as he had an appointment with the COO of a large organization in Pretoria the next morning. He said that he didn't know, but he would taxi into Pretoria and quickly find a place. At that moment, I invited him to stay at our place, which he graciously accepted. It felt as though I had no other option, as though destiny insisted I offer him a place to stay. We walked down from my home office into my home, where I introduced my wife to our guest (fortunately my wife is someone that hosts at the drop of a hat).

Because my son is a real fan of Scooby Doo and he recently watched an episode where Scooby and his friends went to Mexico, my wife called our then 5-year-old son to the living room. He walked in and greeted Al like I have never seen him greet anyone before. He was the perfect child and remembered everything we'd ever taught him. What happened next somehow ventured into the realm of 'what you are'. Al went down onto one knee and took my son by the hand while speaking to him. He did this so naturally and so unpretentiously that we knew this was 'what he is' and not pretends to be! He explained to my son that in his country people often hug when they greet, and he softly hugged him.

Al stayed with us for two nights and during that time I watched him closely. Was he perfect? No. Was he simple? Yes. He showered in cold water. He ate anything and everything. He gave the impression of not judging anyone, because he really sees people as unique, different and complex. My impression was that he really does not get angry; he does what he believes is right and not what others may approve of; he knows what he values—his family relationships, making a difference, and so on. He is fearless.

Over a period of close on two days, he shared with me principles of success that he has shared with many other people in different countries. To be honest, many or even most of the principles I already understood to a lesser or larger degree, as this is actually the field in which I operate on a daily basis. But, being with him moved me! I wanted to be what I taught and shared just a little bit more. I didn't want anger to block my potential any longer. I didn't want to perform below my potential! More than ever, I wanted to do things because they were right and not because doing them would impress others. More than ever before, the example of other great leaders, who have 'become' what they teach, mattered to me! Why? When a leader 'is' what he teaches or requires of others, he moves people much more effectively.

What you say and what you do does not matter as much as what you are—TiLi!

Al could not find space on a luxury bus back to Phalaborwa, so he insisted I drop him off at the nearest taxi rank, where he caught a minibus taxi back to his home.

While in Somerset West, Cape Town, on a business trip, I made the following note in my journal regarding this principle:

"A thought occurs to me that is not new or ground-breaking, but true. These so-called great leaders of society that I meet are almost always asked what makes a great leader. Without fail they give some sort of answer. But, that answer means nothing in comparison to what they actually do, and hopefully are. What Steve Ross, CEO of Edcon, does by bringing his HR director on to the show with him, what Dr Ali Bacher does in being incredibly open and honest as a person, what former Judge Willem Heath does in writing a thank-you letter, is what impresses most. The effect of their good answers faded away long before the effect of their actions and what they really are—humble, open, honest and thoughtful."

As a leader, you will grow towards your destiny of becoming a greater leader in three stages:

1) Say

2) Do

3) Become

Firstly, you will say that you want to do something—I want to be a better leader as a father, husband, manager, and so on. But, you do very little—you are all talk. Then you start realising that you have to start doing something if you ever want to become a greater leader. As you start doing over and over and over, you start entering the final stage of life—you become! By simply being who you are, you will have a greater effect on influencing others, rather than telling (saying) or even doing. People sense whether what you do is because you are in stage two of your growth or because you are in stage three. You see, there is a quantum leap from what your actions are to who you are as a person. Actions can be acted out because you know intellectually you need to act in that way in order to accomplish something. If you have 'become' you will act in the same way, but others can detect sincerity, genuineness and authenticity.

If you scrutinize yourself for a moment, you will realize that you probably move around in all three of these stages. Some standards of behaviour and performance are at the 'say' stage; for others you have started 'doing' something; and yet others have 'become' a part of you. For example, regular exercising may be at 'say' stage; qualifying yourself or an attitude of regularly up-skilling yourself may be at 'do' stage; being a good listener may be in 'become' stage. If you are not moving along the three stages with one of your standards of behaviour, then consider the Law of Movement. Ask yourself why you are not moving forward. There is probably not sufficient movement because you are not really motivated enough, or you don't know how; in other words, the direction is not clear. Perhaps you don't have the necessary structures or resources to create final movement; or you are allowing the Law of Resistance to break you, rather than make you.

When all is said and done, life is simple, but difficult—TiLi! All we have to do is evaluate and do! Can it be simpler than this? I don't think so. Evaluate the facts; evaluate and confront the constraints; evaluate the positives and opportunities; evaluate and commit to the positive aspirations that you will do; evaluate and commit to the directions that you will move in that will get you to your aspirations and address the constraints; evaluate and commit to the structures that you will put into place (do) to get you to your aspirations and directions; act tough or adjust when things are not going according to plan; evaluate—assess and measure—all the directions and structures regularly; surround yourself with the best; become confident in a technical field, dealing with people and engaging life; and remember that what you say and do does not matter as much as who you are.

Lessons learned

In my opinion, to become a great leader in South Africa is more challenging than in most other countries. As the former CEO of Virgin Mobile said to me before our interview, "SA is the real experiment!"

He is so right! South Africa is truly a microcosm of the rest of the world. The world is watching, or should watch our leaders closely as they turn and face our challenges and take a run at them!

What skills should you therefore work towards if your destiny is to become a great leader?

- Define situations factually.
- Confront perceived negatives or constraints to movement.
- See possibilities.
- Create movement through unity (integration).
- Do the tough things.
- Evaluate and re-evaluate fanatically.
- Surround yourself with the best.
- Become confident in the three areas of technical, people and life.

"What you say and do does not matter as much as who you are. As a leader you will grow towards your destiny of great leadership in 3 stages: 1) Say 2) Do 3) Become"

REFERENCES

Andersen, Roy—personal interview as CEO of Liberty Group and non-executive chairman of other organizations
Ashfield, Grant—Leadershipworks
Barry, John—personal interview as founder Adcorp
Clark, Ivan—personal interview as CEO of Grindrod
Cockerill, Ian—personal interview as CEO of Gold Fields Ltd
Covey, Dr Stephen—author
Creamer, Tom—Telesure
Donnelly, Sean—executive director of Moditure
Gore, Adrian—radio interview as CEO of Discovery Health
Hall, Colin—personal interview as former CEO of Wooltru
Khoza, Dr Reuel—chairman Aka Capital (Pty) Ltd, Corobrik (Pty) Ltd, Nedbank Group, Murray and Roberts Cementation and the NEPAD Business Foundation
Laburn, Pete—leadership consultant
Lamberti, Mark—founder of Massmart
Leon, Tony—radio interview, 23 February 2006
Letele, Nolo—personal interview as CEO of Multichoice
Lopez, Alfonzo—author and coach
Loubser, Russell—personal interview as CEO of JSE
McLean, Jim—personal interview as MD of Liberty Properties
Meyer, Heyneke—Blue Bulls rugby coach
Mojela, Louisa—personal interview as CEO of Wiphold
Mokgosi, Thoko—radio interview as CEO of HP

Noko, David—personal interview as CEO of De Beers Consolidated Mines
Nxasana, Sizwe—personal interview as CEO of FirstRand Bank
Oaks, Robert C.—personal interview as retired general and corporate leader
Phosa, Dr Matthews—businessman and ANC treasurer
Pretorius, Brand—personal interview as CEO of McCarthy
Saad, Stephen—Aspen
Saravanja, Marko—personal interview as founder of Regenesys Business School
Summers, Sean—personal interview as CEO of Pick 'n Pay
Wakeford, Kevin—personal interview as CEO of SACOB
Wilford, Colin—as clinical psychologist and executive coach
Woolfson, Alan—personal interview as MD of Charter Life

Coleman, D. (1995). *Emotional Intelligence*, Bloomsbury publishing, London, UK
Ensign Magazine (May 2004)

Leadership Platform services and contact details

We are thought-leaders and consultants in:

- Accelerating leadership learning
- Generating unity in relationships and teams
- Accelerating movement of strategic projects
- Serving the office of the leader
- Showing best return on development return
- Demonstrating unequalled leadership growth

"Take advantage of your exclusive privilege to master the art of moving people and situations profitably"

Empower yourself with Leadership Platform universal laws and models. Contact us on:

Tel: +27 (0)12 653-3022/0604
Fax: +27 (0)86 672-3586
E-mail: info@leadershipplatform.co.za
Website: www.leadershipplatform.com